M000014380

The Diamond Project

Cynthia Hurst

For Wendie —
I hope this will
give you a laugh,
a sentimental tear,
+ chee through
troubled times.
Cynthia Hurst

The Diamond Project

Copyright © 2010 by Cynthia Hurst

All rights reserved. No part of this book may be used or reproduced by any means, graphic, electronic, or mechanical, including photocopying, recording, taping or by any information storage retrieval system without the written permission of the author except in the case of brief quotations embodied in critical articles and reviews.

ISBN: 978-0-9844198-6-9

Printed in the United States of America

Views expressed in this book are solely those of the individual writers.

Send written inquiries to:
P.O. Box 6400, Vero Beach, Florida 32961
For electronic inquiries: www.cynthiahurst.com

This is a work of nonfiction. Any inaccuracies are unintentional. A few names, people and places have been changed to protect individual privacy.

Published by: WRB Publishing
Palm City, Florida
wrb1174@att.net

FIRST EDITION

For Lydia, Winifred, Lillian, Julia, and Julie
In memoriam

Acknowledgments

First and foremost, thank you to every woman who contributed. Without your writings and your assistance there would be no book. I contacted over one hundred remarkable women I personally know with an invitation to write. Seventy-five responded with a Yes. Forty-five actually wrote something. It seems as though they were meant to be part of this project. Their stories are dramatically different, yet interweave in a tapestry of jewel-colored threads that form a striking picture of women today.

Cynthia Grabenbauer was an endless supply of helpful comments, publishing information, book promotion and support in her capacity as publicity director for the Vero Beach BookCenter. Thanks also for the occasional glass of wine together.

Michael Partington does my website and is a computer genius extraordinaire. You were a great help with cover design and technical advice.

A debt of gratitude is owed to Charlotte Claar, Joyce Levi and Kathleen Delis, all of whom agreed to edit and proofread the manuscript.

My husband, Richard, is always in the background lending support, encouragement and thoughtful suggestions. He gives me diamonds literally and figuratively. *Mais oui, merci!*

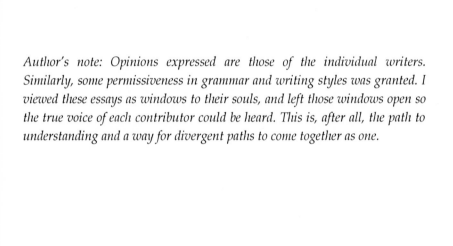

Author's note: Opinions expressed are those of the individual writers. Similarly, some permissiveness in grammar and writing styles was granted. I viewed these essays as windows to their souls, and left those windows open so the true voice of each contributor could be heard. This is, after all, the path to understanding and a way for divergent paths to come together as one.

Contents & Contributors

Foreword
The story of Margrit Szipl, whose mother buried a diamond heirloom in bread she was baking as soldiers beat down their farmhouse door in war-torn Germany. And other diamonds…

Found in Translation   Amy Cox
A former cook on sailing ships and yachts moves to a small French village in Brittany and learns how friendship transcends language.

A Letter from Portugal   Aniza Omar
An enthusiastic young woman writes about living in Portugal and working at the pousadas (historical luxury hotels). Career aspirations, willingness to change, and luck.

The Boys Store   Ann Taylor
Dreams, determination, and successes from the editor of *Vero Beach Magazine*—and talks with her son about the facts of life.

Deo Gratias   Beverly Boyce
On the blessings, adventures, and practicality of raising twelve children, written with a little nostalgia and a lot of love.

May They Run in Heaven   Caroline Wismer
The poignant experiences of a woman who volunteers at a home for profoundly disabled children, describing her emotions and the true meaning of heavenly rest.

More Than Meets the Eye — Carolyn Lineberry
A blue-eyed blond American teacher with intelligence and sensitivity building cultural bridges at an Arab school in Dearborn, Michigan.

The Accidental Tour Guide — Charlotte Claar
A humorous look at three sisters spending a weekend in Paris, and the feelings of independence and exuberance that result.

The Brightness of Being — Christina Fratcher
An RN who opens a quilt shop with practical humor, panache, and lots of color; what we can learn from yard sales. And hey, she's Italian!

E-mail Exchange — Cindy Meier
Correspondence between two very busy women, focusing on a nurse practitioner who builds a fabulous house and gardens on a former Florida orange grove.

The Art of Reinventing Yourself — Devin Reed
An impressive young woman continually reinvents herself — from pop music to banking — as she pursues different paths on the ever-changing road to creating her own life.

Dialogue in Black and White — Diane Halpin
On growing up in Detroit during the '60s, the effects of the riots and the Civil Rights Movement on one young girl, and a friendship that changes everything.

Two Defining Hours — Reverend Elizabeth H. Frazier
Words from one of the first female graduates of the Yale Divinity School, a retired ordained minister takes time after nearly a century to talk about politics and the Power she serves.

Déjà vu Iran   Ellen M. Rantz

A chance meeting in Florida leads to a common bond and memories for a woman from Plymouth, Massachusetts, who lived in the holy city of Mashad, Iran over thirty years ago.

It's Greek to Me   Erasmia Vlastos Novotny

A Greek girl growing up in Detroit travels to the Isle of Crete, discovers her own heritage, and develops a passion to bring cultural pride into her everyday life.

Diamond Mosaic   Gail Jaffe Satuloff

The struggle for perfection and worthiness from a Miami native and former psychotherapist turned yoga instructor, artist and illustrator; served with just the right touch of glitz.

O Pioneer?   J.J. Wilson

Early history of the Feminist Movement through the eyes of a pioneer of Vero Beach, Florida as she started the first women's studies program at Sonoma State University in California.

The Earth Mother   Josephine Hurst

The amazing life and dual career of a marine biologist and cancer researcher, and an artist specializing in sculpture and equestrian art, who lived on a sailboat and flew her own plane.

A Little Stardust in Our Lives   Joyce Levi

At age 81, the writer shows a behind-the-scenes look at thirty years in theatre, from Birmingham to Broadway and beyond, in a life filled with stardust.

Pregnant Pause   **Katie McGinnes**
The hilarious notes from the desk of a first-time mother describing her experiences during pregnancy and preparations for her newborn daughter.

Moonlight Sonata   **Kim Huston**
Soft notes from a piano teacher in Haslett, Michigan. The power of music; the joy she brings to her students — and to the parents who hear them play.

Quadratic Equation   **Kristy Rapley**
Gripping story of a quadriplegic living in Bakersfield, California, working for a major oil company and as a motivational speaker for disabled students — and how she got there.

My Life in Belgium   **Laurence Lefebvre**
The Secrétaire (administrator) of a major health and social services organization in Mouscron, Belgium, shares a typical week in her life of work and family. *Translated from the French*

Freelance Writer on the Treasure Coast
                                        Leona DeRosa Bodie
A children's book author who writes an adult pirate adventure; and describes her inspirations and influences along the way.

A Villa in Italy   **Linda Lovisa**
Summer times at a family retreat in Cavasso Nuovo, Italy, an area in the northeast of "the boot" known for Alpine beauty, prosciutto ham and exquisite tile-making.

My Dear Jack   **Lynda Tissington**
An English woman, recently widowed, writes a love letter to her husband, Jack; and shares the closeness and continuity of family scattered in America, England, Ireland and Australia.

My American Fairy Tale   **Lyne Hebig**
A French-Canadian woman resettles in Plano, Texas, and dreams come true. With humility and lightness of being, she tells the story of her "transplantation" from Canada to the U.S.A.

Leave It to Cupid   **Marianne Heimerl-Montague**
The scandalous tale of three husbands, and the undying search for love from a woman who was born in Germany, grew up in Switzerland, lives in America, and loves Cupid.

On ne choisit pas qui on est mais qui on devient
                                    Marion Hottier
One Does Not Choose Who One Is but Who One Becomes
A thirteen-year-old French girl talks about growing up on a farm outside a small village and her first impressions of America. *Translated from the French*

Prairie Skies to PowerPoint   **Marlowe Olson Arnold**
The joys of a career in teaching from a woman born in North Dakota who became a children's librarian and an adjunct instructor in English at Indian River State College in Florida.

The Queen of Heartless   **Marsha Foresman**
Exposé about the 500+ people fired as a result of employee rule infractions and the resultant head-chopping. Actually, it's about human folly and your tax dollars…

On Engineering Climate Control Systems   Martha Nefcy
or Is it Hot in Here? Is it Cold in Here?
The struggles and successes of an executive in the male-dominated field of design engineering for the automotive industry; and an interesting lesson in golf with Japanese businessmen.

Mary Ellen the Clown   Mary Ellen Clark
Started as a family lark, a woman becomes a professional clown. She learns make-up, juggling, balloon animals; the art of entertaining and the magic of showbiz.

The Purple Teapot   Melissa S. Kerley, Ph.D.
A recounting of overcoming physical challenges, recognizing our limitations, and realizing dreams from someone who went on to earn a Ph.D., and found a purple teapot.

Gateways   Merana Cadorette
From a Girl Scout history coloring book to a book of watercolors illustrating Georgia portals and garden entrances, this author and artist finds gateways to life.

Loving to Listen   Paige Fortner
Working in a sophisticated spa and beauty boutique, this hair designer is not only an expert stylist but an excellent listener. She offers some useful tips.

But You Don't *Look* Like a Warden   Pamela K. Withrow
Stories from the first female warden in the 115-year history of the Michigan Reformatory, a maximum security prison for men. On being a trailblazer.

Swimming in a Sea of Men   Pauline Nefcy

A woman in Seattle, Washington, talks about her career in the traditionally men-only field of accounting, and offers tips for success based on her experiences (with big fish!).

Untitled Kidnapping Story   Rachel Raines

A young aspiring actress in Los Angeles, California, uses her talents to survive a kidnapping alive and intact. Written in film noir style.

Change of Course   Rebecca Stimson

The single life as a choice that can bring joy, meaning, and yes, fulfillment, once one stops looking for a Chris-Craft in a rowboat world and realizes we all plot our own course.

Who Said You Can't Hit a Home Run?   Sally Hall

An Ohio businesswoman and her husband, a former friar, adopt two Native American children; the tribes, tribulations and triumphs of work, family…and baseball.

Five O   Soyong Kang Partington

A cultural tale of coming to America from South Korea, becoming a well-known ceramicist and teacher of raku pottery techniques in Indianapolis, and a few foreign spots as well.

Dollars and Sense   Susan Collins

The prosperous middle-class lifestyle afforded by the Detroit auto industry; and how one person learned to stretch a dollar and make ends meet as the boom times declined.

The Entrepreneur   Tanja McGuire

A young, savvy businesswoman in Vero Beach opens not one, but two successful boutique-spas on the posh Ocean Drive in the midst of hurricane recovery and an economic downturn.

Too Busy for Bees   Teresa Forshag

A Tacoma, Washington wife and mother with attitude who takes in foster babies, works as a nurse practitioner and court advocate for abused and neglected children…and raises bees.

Finding My Strength   Tiffany Vincent

A high school student helps her mother through difficult times and finds her own strength. Now a college student, she desires rewarding work and dreams of a lipstick line called *lippity slicks*.

What Color Do You Want to Be?   Jennifer Suzanne Boyce

A thirty-something sister talks about problems and experiences unique to her generation, makes the decision to play the game of Life, and finds hope for the future in an 80-year-old redhead.

Foreword

During the Second World War, my neighbor and dear friend Margrit was a young girl living in Germany in the area then known as East Prussia. Russian soldiers were invading the farms and villages, capturing or beating any remaining men, raping the women, and stealing everything they could. Margrit lived on one of the many rolling farms that supplied corn to the region. To protect Margrit, her mother told the soldiers her daughter had TB. She was, in fact, in her bed that day, coughing and sickly. The ruse worked. (Her pretty older sister was not so fortunate, but she survived the indignities thrust upon her nonetheless.)

Margrit's mother was baking bread when the soldiers broke down their door. She wore a family heirloom, an exquisite diamond ring in a pear-shaped setting. As the soldiers entered the house, she quickly buried the ring in the dough and baked it with the bread. Today Margrit is the only survivor. And the ring, which she wears now, is her memento, a reminder of what she is made of.

The idea for this book came to me one day as I thought about Margrit and the many facets of the many women I know. Everyone has a story. What drew me to this project was the connection these individual stories have to our own, the spark of recognition that says, "Why, this could be me." *I am not alone.*

The writers are intelligent, accomplished, humorous, and spiritual women; ordinary women leading extraordinary lives. They range in age from thirteen to ninety-five. Countries represented include Greece, Belgium, Portugal, South Korea, France, England, and many of these United States. They come from different economic classes, races and creeds. Their voices are heard in a variety of ways, from plain speaking to passionate, practical to total panache. Their stories will surprise you, delight you, and encourage you to challenge yourself, recognize your choices, and be thankful for your blessings. Young women will be inspired by the possibilities available to them; older women will have faith restored, as it is clear their contributions have been remarkable and their lessons have not been forgotten.

Every woman who participated in this project wrote for the sheer joy of it, without the promise of fortune or fame or financial gain. They shared their stories so *others* might benefit. The excitement generated from this project was a reward in itself. To see so many of the contributors blossom as they realized heretofore unknown dimensions of themselves was another unexpected result. And it was fun.

The evolution of consciousness fascinates me. What inspired individuals like the primitive cave painter(s) of Lascaux, Leonardo da Vinci, Galileo, Queen Elizabeth I, or Amelia Earhart, so far ahead of their contemporaries? What makes the ideas and inventions of Stephen Hawking, Gloria Steinem, Pablo Picasso, Yo-Yo Ma, Ella Fitzgerald, Bill Gates, or Queen Rania Al Abdullah of Jordon resonate with the times? How does a new development catch on and endure? In the modern technological age, change is rapid and fame is fleeting. Of the latest *TIME 100* list of the world's most influential people, I recognized less than half of the names, though reading about them jogged my mind on several. In a recent issue of *Popular Mechanics* I picked up on a plane, I was astounded at the developments, from high tech one-person flying machines to the latest Bentley (all 400 pre-ordered and on reserve at $285,000 each).

Innovation continues. Art cannot be stopped. One thing is certain: all creative minds and hearts ignite the collective consciousness and move us all forward socially, scientifically, and spiritually. There is a light to all of it, a divine aspect that cannot be denied.

On another level, my husband tells me a humorous story about a man who worked in the diamond mines and left the mine each day with a wheelbarrow full of sand. Each day the sand would be sifted and inspected for contraband, but nothing was ever found. Months after the laborer retired quite comfortably, a former guard met the man in a café one day and asked, "I know you were stealing, but how did you do it?"

"I was stealing wheelbarrows," the man replied.

I don't recommend stealing anything, but I like the idea of the obvious sight that goes unseen; the simple struggle that goes into everyday living and emerges triumphant. And who knows of the jewels out there, buried in a pan of rising bread or emerging from the mine, hidden with all the patience and cleverness we possess, ready to be worn proudly when the time is right?

Thus, it is my pleasure to present to you a few of these diamonds in the rough, uncut stones, polished gems, engagement rings and antique settings that have withstood the test of time. The facets come together individually and collectively, complete with cut, color, clarity, and carat—genuine diamonds all.

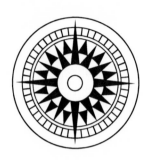

Found in Translation

Amy Cox

Amy Cox is a woman of independent means. She seems to absolutely love life. Young and exuberant, she completely updated her cement block house, built on the Citrus Isles of Fort Lauderdale in the late 50s and purchased in 2002, with big comfy furniture, sponge painted walls, renovated baths, and a shower outside by the pool. A riot of flowers surrounds the front entrance. Husband Michael is a boat captain, sailing the world. During his long absences, she cared for her pets, built a block party of new neighbors and friends, and kept the home fires burning. Together they welcomed their first child, a daughter, and moved to some fantastic places, including a stint in the Brittany region of France. Amy learned some lessons along the way. She has anecdotes both interesting and entertaining. Enjoy!

There was so much to do to prepare. Although I had recently given birth to my first and only child, I had to pack the contents of the house into storage to prepare for a two-year move, then take the dog, cat and two-month-old to Concarneau, a small fishing village in Brittany, France; yet somehow I was undaunted. After all, the previous decade working on board sailing yachts as a chef, with my husband as captain, had trained me to deal with tight scheduling and multitasking. That must be why I decided I also needed to have a garage sale on the Labor Day weekend.

And I'd have to say it was all going well. My sister-in-law was in town to help, although she had her eleven- and two-year-old along also. We were getting the house packed up and managing to entertain the children. A garage sale seemed like a perfect idea to divest ourselves of "stuff." That was before Hurricane Frances hit. With the power out and a lot more things to pack up, the whole idea of moving seemed ridiculous. Was it postnatal hormones taking over? What HAD I been thinking?! I'm not sure how we managed it, but we moved out of our house in time to vacate for our new tenants. And we managed to have a day of R&R at the pet friendly Beach Motel before flying on to France.

Living and working as professional crew on yachts prepares one for having to move to numerous places on short or often unknown time frames. But this time we were prepared for this new venture. Mike had been working in Concarneau for nearly a year already and we had even been over there previously (with the cat and dog) during the first trimester of my pregnancy to set up our little cottage. Mike had done a superb job of selecting us a quaint old stone cottage in an old section of the village, right next to the coastline. Together we had furnished the 3-bed/1½ bath house, set up all of the utilities, and then set about to explore our new turf.

Mike has a fairly good working knowledge of French, but, having been raised in California, I had opted to learn Spanish. It never ceased to amaze me how Spanish would come out when I tried speaking French! That took some time and effort to get over, but eventually I managed to utter halting French. I never did become anywhere near fluent. Still, it's more than just the language that sets our countries apart—there is a world of culture that I never knew was so drastically different. It was this difference that I struggled with each day, to try and find my place, for the most part alone, with an infant.

So as Mike set out to work each morning, my daughter and I would attempt to set about our day, buying groceries, preparing meals, going for walks, and eventually integrating. Of course, as I no longer had the luxury of holing up with assistance from my friends or family, I did the only thing I knew how to do —organize and schedule my daughter. It wasn't until she was four months old that I had this under control, but by then it was mid-November and she was eating some solids and sleeping through the night. This meant that I could now venture out without fear of infant meltdown while my self-confidence dissolved as the French women nodded knowingly and clucked at me (real or imagined!).

In our earlier visit to France, I had made an unlikely friend with Mike's shipyard colleague's mother-in-law, Patricia. This elderly woman had befriended me and my dog. She nursed her sickly husband and missed the dogs of her youth, and she enjoyed the companionship we gave each other as we would walk along the beach with the stroller and a romping canine. We couldn't communicate much, but we spent hours together every week walking, enjoying tea and pastries. Eventually her daughter (the colleague's wife) and the grandchildren joined us. We spent our afternoons exchanging recipes as we baked chocolate chip cookies and Breton cakes. Patricia even looked after the dog on the odd weekend, allowing us to leave town and explore France. Upon our return to France with the new family, we renewed our friendship.

Now that my daughter's schedule was more predictable, I set out to join a local Mom's gathering. Well, sort of local — all right, I had to drive 35 minutes to the next local village and it took me three times to actually find it, but it at least gave me something to do every other Tuesday. No, no one spoke English and my French still left everything to be desired, but I sat with the others and watched them interact with their children. I came to learn that, beyond that limited interaction, the main thing missing in my new life as a mother was that I had no one to talk to about issues, concerns, thoughts, etc. Of course, my husband was very supportive and we spent as much time as possible with him. We would walk to his office daily as it was two minutes from home; and not only did he join us for lunch every day, but we often chided him to come home a little earlier than he would have liked. Still, nothing quite replaces the female nattering or clucking that goes on about mothering and its challenges.

So I continued to explore and reach out to new friends and experiences, but I also managed to cast a line back home to Florida through the blessed invention of e-mail. My line was picked up by a friend of a friend whom I barely knew, but who, like me, had decided to have a baby slightly later in life. Her lengthy e-mails and inquisitive views offered the maternal lifeline that I so lacked. She rescued me as it turns out, but more on that later.

In January, four months into our move to the northern coast of Brittany, I found a small business card posted on the corner of the bulletin board of our local *boulangerie*. Her name was Lisa and she taught English. EUREKA, someone I can actually speak to! Anyone named Lisa had to be a native English speaker I thought, but the voice on the answering machine would challenge that. To my surprise and pleasure, Lisa turned out to be a Puerto Rican-American, raised in Brooklyn. She had married a Breton, had two sons and had immigrated to Concarneau. She spoke fluent French, Spanish and, of course, English and we quickly became friends. Not only did she help me learn more French, but she held some English classes at our house for advanced students hopeful to learn the colloquialisms of our language. Moreover, she was excited to be speaking English herself as the opportunities were very limited in this part of the country. Lisa helped explain many of the cultural gaps that we couldn't bridge; through her we came to learn more of the Breton ways—a very tight knit community, almost cliquish.

Unfortunately, while my social life began to grow, Mike's work life was deteriorating. Cultural differences, the financial pressures borne by the shipyard, and the strain from the yard's steep learning curve led to the ultimate demise of the working relationship between Mike and his previously friendly colleague. In February, regrettably, this man gave instruction to his wife to sever all relations with me, and this tumbled downhill to his mother-in-law who felt she needed to follow her daughter. To this day I cannot understand the man's reasoning, but I was told that he was a *Breton* man, "they have their ways and they are not to be dismissed."

By the beginning of spring, work relations had become untenable for Mike, and for the well-being of the project he decided to resign in May. The following month we left our cottage and the small life we had begun to build there. Somehow we had made it through the cold, often lonely winter, only to find that as the weather warmed and the flowers bloomed, the climate was still chilly for us. Upon our return to Florida we felt broken and lost.

But my lifeline, who had exchanged so many e-mails with me, continued to provide us with support. Extending her home to us and offering her full friendship, Renee brought home the most important idea that yachting all around the world had failed to teach me. Companionship, having friends with common interests, can ground you and bind you more securely to any place than bricks and mortar. I can live anywhere in the world if I have friends.

A Letter from Portugal

Aniza Omar

Aniza Omar lives in Portugal. I first met her while staying at the Pousada de Queluz/Lisbon. Wearing a dark skirt and crisp white blouse, her long black hair in a neat bun, she was at once a bespectacled school girl and a concierge professional. One night, as my husband and I returned from an evening of fado music, Aniza was waiting with a glass of tawny port. She had remained on her shift at the hotel past midnight so she could greet us and say goodnight, as we were leaving the following morning. Now we are facebook friends, in touch on a regular basis. Aniza has a remarkable spirit. I have made few changes to her missive, written in the form of a letter to me, in an attempt to let her voice shine through. Her first language is Portuguese, not English, so this was not particularly easy for her. I sign off as Aniza always does with me: Beijinhos *(little kisses).*

Dear Cindy,

First of all I would like to thank you for choosing me for your great new Project. Finally I have some time and I was thinking of the themes that you gave. I'm going to make a resume about who I am and if you need some more information feel free to say. I know that you told all the participants that they don't need to get too personal in talking about their lives, but it's your project so I think it's important to be as much sincere as you can.

Here I Go.

Who I am:

Aniza Omar, I'm 30 years old. I was born in Mozambique and living in Portugal since I was five. I am Muslim but not very much of a practitioner of my faith. I'm single (and I have to say I love my space—probably that's why I haven't settled down yet). I'm very Impulsive and I hate Injustice of any kind. I LOVE MUSIC and I'm a Huge fan of U2. I love soccer and my team is BENFICA (this year we will be Champions yupiii!). I'm not so ambitious. I live one day at a time. I have one brother and one sister. My parents are divorced and I have three beautiful nephews and one goddaughter. She is beautiful too, and we have a special connection. Her name is Beatriz. The man of my life is my first nephew that lives with me since he was two months old, now he is almost five. His name is Fardeen... I've two beautiful dogs (yorkies Nina and Salvador, my babies). I live with my sister and my nephew; and my oldest sister, Fatima (Beatriz's mum), lives nearby. She has an older son, Renato, 15 years old; he is lovely too. Cindy, this is my closest family. My parents are divorced; my mum lives in Mozambique and my dad in London. They got divorced when I was almost 17; tuff time but at the moment they have a cordial relationship just because of us.

Regarding friends, I'm blessed, I've got the Best I could have. My Best friends are from high school and they are split everywhere but it doesn't matter how long we keep each other distant, we always have a thought or a word to say whenever is needed. They are the Best...and make me proud to say that we are friends since we were 15. I've got Best friends Tania and Sonia; you can see them at my photos in facebook album "Barcelona" (we went there to see a Take That Concert) but — there is always a "but" — I lost a Best friend in October 2001. His name was Roberto Ribeiro; he was my friend and neighbor since I was five. He committed suicide when he was 20 years old. He was going through a deep depression. This is one of my biggest losses. I had a big tuff time and I had to ask for medical help to move on. I had the guilt of his death weighing on me (wondering if I had done something).

I have a degree in Public Relations. When I finished high school I went to London to stay with my dad. For three and a half years I studied and worked part time there in a Mexican Restaurant. Great experience I will never forget. I love London and I go often to visit my dad and to see old friends. In London my passion for Restaurants started when I came back to Lisbon. I had been a Manager at the Mexican Restaurant La Siesta. I was blessed, too — I learned a lot about how to make a profit without forgetting the staff that surrounds you, but unfortunately after three years I needed to change to a different thing. Cindy, without thinking a lot, when I was 24 I quit my job and started again.

Do you know how I got the Job in the Pousada?* I was in a Café (in Portugal it's almost a tradition after dinner we go to a café) at 22:00. I saw a request for a waiter in a newspaper, phoned there, and got the interview for the next day. The Manager loved my spirit and I got the Job! You know what is the Best thing about working in Hotels and Pousadas? Every day is different — you never can expect the same from yesterday.

The Pousada was an entrance door to get in the Pestana Group, but my objective was to get a position with the Pestana Palace Hotel where I work now, and I wanted to change from Food and Beverage to Front Office. At the moment I have been working here for almost four years and I really love my Job. (Check Pestana Palace Hotel Lisbon, the hotel is beautiful.)

To finish I would like to thank you once again. I Hope I've helped you for the book. If you need something else let me know.

And remember this is me…

Beijinhos,

Aniza

---

* *Pousadas are over 40 luxury hotels that emphasize rustic character, historical significance and genuine Portuguese hospitality. They are elegant lodgings situated in former castles, palaces, abbeys and monasteries, in areas of great natural beauty, converted into 4-star hotels and restaurants. Formerly run by the state, in 2003 the Pestana Group won a forty-year contract to manage the pousadas.*

The Boys Store

Ann Taylor

Ann Taylor is the picture of sophistication and elegant charm. On the hottest Florida day she appears serene, dressed in a light skirt and linen jacket, her hair pulled back with a simple barrette. This cool competence extends not only to social occasions but to cultural events, community service, and her work as feature writer and editor for the glossy Vero Beach Magazine. *From her missive it is uncertain whether the cool and calm approach always works with family, but what is certain is that Ann will find a way.*

"Why did we have to move?" my daughter asked as we stood in the kitchen surrounded by boxes still unpacked.

"Your father got a promotion and once we get settled we're going to love it here. You'll see," I said, hoping to convince myself as well our 13-year-old.

"But I miss my friends," she sighed, reaching for a hug. As the two of us embraced I realized I felt the same way, yet the optimist in me saw this as an opportunity to make a fresh start. For years I had dreamed of becoming a published writer; instead, encouraged by my parents and teachers I majored in art education and went on to instruct high school students in the fine points of design, which I thoroughly enjoyed. But the dream kept recurring. Maybe this was time I could do something about it.

A week later a notice in the newspaper caught my eye. Caldecott award-winning author Jean Horton Berg was going to teach an eight-week "Writing for Children" course at the local high school starting the following Thursday. It was just what I was looking for.

Jean not only taught us the basics of writing, she encouraged us to let our imaginations soar when she gave us in-class and homework assignments. Mine definitely did and she must have liked what I came up with, because she gave me a scholarship to the Philadelphia Writers' Conference, where "Writing for Your Local Newspaper" was one of the half-day sessions I signed up for. The instructor, a seasoned and enthusiastic journalist, made writing feature stories sound both exciting and demanding. This was what I wanted to try my hand at and I knew just where to get started — *The Suburban and Wayne Times.*

My first step was to schedule a meeting with the editor, a Mr. Bob Butterwick. Unfortunately, it didn't go quite the way I envisioned it would.

"Why are you here?" Butterwick asked as he shuffled through papers scattered across his desk.

"I want to write for your newspaper," I replied, with a cheerful smile.

"You and everybody else," he harrumphed, peering at me over his glasses. "So what have you got?"

"What do you mean what have I got?"

"Unless you've brought me a couple of story leads, which I don't think you have, there's nothing I can offer you even if I wanted to. Come back tomorrow, same time, with three ideas and I'll see if I like any of them. Then we'll talk."

Determined to show him I was serious, I poured through every page of *The Suburban*, culling bits and pieces of information until I came up with three possibilities. The next day I was back knocking on his door.

"What are you doing here?" Butterwick asked, staring at me as though I had just sprouted a second head.

"You told me to come back today with three suggestions so here I am and here they are," I said, handing him my list.

Butterwick only liked one of my ideas but that was all it took. I had my first assignment and my first deadline. It took me three days to write a 500-word article and when I saw it in print with my name underneath the headline, I was elated. No matter that the story had been heavily edited or that it was on the last page of the sports section just before the automobile sales; I was now a bona fide published writer.

I kept going into Butterwick's office armed with article ideas and soon he started giving me assignments. The writing came easier and I learned from the editorial changes until they became fewer and fewer. It wasn't long before my articles—and my byline—had moved to the lifestyle section, a few even landing on the front page.

When the full-time feature writer resigned eight months after I first walked into his office, Butterwick offered me the job. I could have hugged the old grouch. From then on I was officially on staff with a desk, telephone and business cards plus a multitude of story leads to follow. I interviewed and wrote about people of all ages, from a five-year-old who organized a food drive for the homeless to an 84-year-old who played Christmas carols on his saxophone at the post office every December. Life was good.

It got even better when Butterwick gave his blessing after I asked him if I could write a weekly column that would be upbeat and humorous. I titled it "Something to Say." The fodder was my family and they supplied me with an endless stream of subject matter. This one, tweaked slightly since it was first published, has always been one of my favorites.

"The Facts of Life"

I know I was told about them, but I can't seem to recall the scene or the script. No need to worry, thought I. When it comes time to tell my offspring about the birds and the bees I'd do it right, none of the beating-around-the-bush, the stork brought you bit.

"Where did I come from?" my son first asked when he was four.

Having done extensive research on the importance of parents being open, honest and forthright in all matters pertaining to the facts of life, I didn't hesitate.

"From the Boys Store, third shelf, and you cost $3.98!" The words were out of my mouth before I could stop them.

He looked up at me with those trusting brown eyes of his and smiled, satisfied with my answer.

I breathed uneasily for a couple of years.

"Mom, where did you tell me I came from?" my son asked when he was seven.

"From the Boys Store, remember? We were really lucky to get you — you were the cutest, most wonderful baby on the fourth shelf."

"I thought it was the third shelf," he said, eyes wide.

"Hmm...let me see," I said, pausing and looking skyward as if in great thought. I was actually trying to buy time in the hope he'd forget the whole thing, dash outside and hop on his bicycle. No such luck. He just stood there and waited.

"You're absolutely right!" I exclaimed, snapping my fingers. "It was the third shelf. I remember now because it was about here..." I patted an imaginary shelf with my hand, "You really were the cutest, most wonderful little boy in the entire store!"

With that he smiled, went outside and hopped on his bike. And with that I went back to my parenting book, nervously pouring through each page. Next time the question comes up it's honesty all the way."

That time came sooner than I had thought.

"Mom, tell me more about the Boys Store."

"What Boys Store?" I asked while mashing potatoes for dinner.

"You know, the Boys Store!"

My heart caught in my throat, my legs felt wobbly and pieces of potatoes flew when I dropped the electric mixer.

"Ah, that store, sure," I said, trying to look cool and confident. This was it, I told myself. Be open. Be honest.

"Well, it was crowded that day and there were all these shelves full of little boys in blue blankets." I just couldn't help myself. "The minute I saw you I said to your father, there he is! He's the one! I dashed over to the third shelf, scooped you up, paid $5.98 and you were ours!"

Silence.

"Wait a minute, Mom. I thought I only cost $3.98."

"Inflation!"

"Oh."

A great deal of serious talk has gone on since then, but we haven't forgotten the Boys Store. Just yesterday my son, who now has tiny wisps of hair beginning to appear on his upper lip, said, "You know, Mom, I really liked it when you told me about the Boys Store. The other guys were always talking about some stork and there I was, telling them about the third shelf and inflation. You'd probably have to pay at least $9.98 for me today."

Now that's a fact of life!

It was written almost 30 years plus two more moves ago and I've been penning human interest articles and columns for newspapers and magazines ever since. At last count the number was well over 3,000.

I often think about Butterwick who gave me my start and I'll never forget the surprised look on his face or what he said that day I reappeared in his office with those three story ideas.

"No one else has ever come back."

Thank heavens I did.

Deo Gratias

Beverly Boyce

Beverly Boyce is my mother. She knows each of her children profoundly and has always chosen to understand rather than criticize. She wrote something typically simple, practical, humble, and humorous, with a touch of nostalgia. I didn't want to change a thing. Mom doesn't tell you about our being Catholic (with twelve children, perhaps it goes without saying), or that we grew up in the house where she still lives, but it doesn't really matter. Our solid foundation and our faith in family came from the abundant love between her and my dad.

I was asked to write about the challenges of raising a large family of twelve children—difficult in any era, always fraught with the age-old problems and some unique to the times. I had my first baby in late 1952 and my last in mid-1973. The first thing I did that gave us a good start was to pick a wonderful husband and father for my children. My children all agree (for once) on that and I see the strong influence that he had in their lives.

I was, in today's jargon, a stay-at-home mom. I wasn't special, this was the norm. Dad went to work; Mom stayed home to run the household and care for the children. Babies and toddlers didn't go to day care, nursery school, pre-school, or anything else until kindergarten...also the norm. Disposable diapers at this time were pretty uncommon and of poor quality, so I raised my twelve children mostly using cloth diapers. Disposables were used at this time, but usually just for vacations, long car rides or outings. I didn't discover them until my last baby was born, and I thought they were wonderful, much improved by that time. I never heard the expression "play date" when my children were small. They had playmates at home (plenty of them!) and in the neighborhood. Our home had a nice park nearby, with supervised activities and games on certain days. The children went to the neighborhood school the first years, but eventually as they grew older we had a car pool. I, too, had friends in the neighborhood and had my share of coffee klatches while the children played in the backyard. This was my support group.

People asked how we fed such a group on one paycheck (thank you, Ford Motor Company). Sometimes I wonder myself, but somehow we always did. I cooked dinner every night and we did not order pizza or Chinese food or anything else. It really wasn't done much then. (If, for working families today it relieves stress and keeps the home fires burning, I say go for it.) When the family started getting smaller as the children grew up and left home, I found myself making big pots of chili, spaghetti, or stew and then eating leftovers for days.

In the early years before we had a second car, I grocery shopped on the weekends when my husband was home from the office. But often the markets came to us. We had a milkman (a thing of the past), but when we ran low on milk I would sometimes mix some powdered milk with water to make enough to stretch our supply. We also had a Sanders man (bread and baked goods), a Fuller Brush Man (cleaning products), and a fruit and vegetable vendor who regularly traversed the neighborhood in spring and summer. The Good Humor truck came around in the hot weather and occasionally we would have a treat, nickel sticks for the kids and an ice cream bar for Mom and Dad.

We were fortunate to have four loving grandparents living nearby. They visited often and rarely came empty-handed—a bag of fresh fruit, some bread or coffee cake, etc. One time, their grandfather took four of the boys to the barber shop after witnessing the awful job my husband had done with the clippers! We did have to struggle at times, especially when Ford Motor Company went on strike twice. As they got a little older the boys had paper routes and the girls babysat, which helped out.

As with most families, we had our share of illness to deal with. We had four boys with mumps at the same time. What a sight! There was no shot for measles, mumps or chicken pox then but luckily the illnesses ran their course and there were no long-term effects. Two of the kids had scarlet fever and three had appendicitis at different times. In one case, the appendix burst and my son Christopher, age thirteen at the time, was very sick for about four weeks. I'm thankful everything had a good outcome. Of course, there were always trips to the doctor, dentist, and optometrist (most of the children inherited my nearsightedness), but nothing out of the ordinary really. Braces were not a rite of passage as they are today, so no orthodontist appointments. Fortunately, the children had pretty straight teeth.

Our family car was a large station wagon, a popular choice then for large families since there were no minivans yet. With my husband at the wheel, the baby in my lap (a definite no-no now but no car seats yet) and the other children in the back seats, we were off to the zoo, the lake or the drive-in movie. Drive-ins charged by the car, so we got our money's worth. Cars were not equipped with seatbelts — I shudder to think of it now. The teen years are a source of concern for all parents as they were for us, with the ever-present influences and temptations in our society. One by one they learned to drive a car and eventually, against my better judgment, two motorcycles. Except for a few fender benders, they all came through those years unscathed.

We didn't have the many wonderful technological advantages of today — no cell phones, Internet, e-mail, MySpace, iPod, Google, Giggle (I put that in!), twitter, tweet and others, all a different language to me. These are a great source of learning and information and can help keep families connected but can also be a source of contention and concern. Of course these things should be used to good advantage just as I had some things that my own mother didn't have (a clothes dryer comes to mind). The kids had transistor radios, record players, sports equipment, musical instruments, comic books, assorted pets, and a parade of Barbie dolls. All these things were interspersed with happy times: birthday parties, picnics, holidays and eventually graduations and weddings. So there was a balance.

Some difficulties can be multiplied in a large family. There are more people to care for and make sure nobody gets lost in the shuffle, more housekeeping and cooking, and more of a strain on the budget; it is definitely NOT cheaper by the dozen. Of course, the joys and rewards are multiplied as well. Modern-day mothers who balance babies and budget, home and husband plus a full- or part-time job do something I don't think I could have done, but for my time I did what circumstances demanded and what I saw fit.

Young families are so mobile today, not always living near the family home. They have to pursue job opportunities or are transferred to other states or other countries. My son Dan and his wife, Veronica, (from Ecuador) lived in Mexico City for five years, but are back in the U.S. now. My daughter Michelle and her husband, Joe, lived in Europe for two years, but are also back home now in Michigan. So families today have different challenges to face that I did not; moving away and leaving family and friends behind, traveling to new places, speaking other languages, and more. This can be a new adventure and with travel opportunities available today, families seem to adjust.

We had our ups and downs as everyone does, but our love for each other and our shared faith in God brought us through the peaks and valleys of everyday life. I can truthfully say that I enjoyed raising my children. I had my bad days, of course, but on the whole I never felt trapped, subservient, or unfulfilled. I felt loved, secure, content and blessed.

In my wedding ceremony (way back in February 1952), I remember the priest saying to us in regard to matrimony that "Its joys and sorrows, its pleasures and its pains are hidden from your eyes." This has been true to the end. Now I am a widow and my children are busy raising my many grandchildren. Life has been good. *Deo Gratias.*

May They Run in Heaven

Caroline Wismer

This is a poignant story about the lost and forgotten, in a place we might never think about unless we found ourselves with the predicament of a severely disabled child. Like a prayer, it is the kind of thing that might only come into our awareness when we are in need. But this story is also about the excellent and loving care provided by saintly people right here on this earth, one woman's promise, and the heaven she prays will exist for these children when their time in this world is ended. Caroline did not wish to write directly about herself, but she agreed to share this experience from many years ago.

In the eyes of the casual passerby there would be nothing memorable about the putty-colored concrete block building at the juncture of state road 17 and the broad sycamore-lined avenue leading into the town of Linnville. The single-story structure was composed of three long wings radiating from a hub. A dull pewter grey chain link fence surrounded the building and yard; just outside the fence was an expanse of blacktop for parking. This utile blight rounded out the institutional banality of the scene.

But my eyes were not those of a casual passerby for they had seen beyond those dreary grey walls and into the building's heart; and my memories of that place hang by no slender thread but are engulfed in my mind.

I remember very well the first time ever I pulled into that parking lot for a heavy feeling of dread overpowered me. My urge was to simply drive away. Must I respect my vow? After all, it was a promise made to a *dead* person—one who would never know. *But I would know.* So I stepped from the car and walked into the Linnville Children's Home, an institution for desperately, profoundly disabled children; and when I put my name on the sign-in roster just inside the door, in my heart I wrote the name of that unknown person whose donated corneal tissue had restored the sight in my right eye.

A young lady greeted me warmly and invited me to have a seat in the waiting room while she told the coordinator of volunteers, Jane Dayton, that I was there. I sank into a comfortable chair and felt a perfect fool when I caught myself smiling back at the huge Teddy bear seated across from me. But then, it was a *smiley* sort of room. Bright sunlight streamed through the windows, lifting the spirits and enabling the many live green plants in clay pots to flourish. Fanciful nursery rhyme characters painted in cheerful primary colors paraded around the room in a mural, and there were stuffed toys all around.

I remember thinking how much the children must enjoy this room, but I was naïve. Later I realized this room was not decorated for them, for only a few were even aware of their surroundings. No, not for them, but for the broken-hearted parents who brought the imperfect fruit of their bodies to this place to turn them over to the care of strangers. It was decorated to help then believe they had made the correct decision, for children would surely be lovingly cared for here.

My interview with Miss Dayton must have gone all right, for I was accepted as a volunteer and assigned to schoolroom C.

Conventional wisdom could hardly imagine a schoolroom without chalkboards, desks, pencils, books. And, where were the bulletin boards displaying perfect spelling test papers and the colorful crayon drawings of grass, trees, flowers, with the omnipresent sun shining above the blue line of the sky?

Instead, this schoolroom contained a large water bed, shelves, several chairs designed to hold a child securely, and a number of blue plastic floor mats. There were a few toys as well as some furnishings for the comfort and convenience of the adults.

The toys were seldom used, but sometimes we would hold a child's hand with ours cupped over it and simulate play by guiding that small hand. I liked to do this with the jack-in-the-box, and when we turned the crank together I hoped against hope there would be some reaction when the funny little man with the red-peaked hat and the big hooknose popped out. I was always disappointed.

One of my duties was to feed the children lunch. Those who were able to swallow were spoon-fed soft foods. We strapped the children into their custom-made wheelchairs for eating. These chairs had padded vise-like devices to hold their heads erect. Those who could not eat had plastic tubing surgically inserted into their stomachs or throats; and some had tubes threaded through one nostril. Plastic bags of a gray gruel-like nutritional substance were connected to these tubes and hung from hooks on moveable stands. This type of feeding was continuous, so we watched the flow carefully to see it was not interrupted.

The care these children received was truly remarkable. I never witnessed a shudder of disgust, a shrug of indifference, or an unkind word on the part of anyone—not from the laundress who washed those mounds of soiled diapers, the nurse who gave them such loving care, the director, or any volunteer. This place was a communal cocoon—grey, dreary, ugly on the outside; but a haven for the vulnerable children for whom it was home. But the most memorable aspect of the Linnville Children's Home had to be the children themselves.

Five-year-old Mowamba had coffee-colored skin, huge dark empty eyes, and the mind of an infant. This unfortunate boy had undergone abdominal surgery as a baby and something went wrong with the anesthetic; his brain was deprived of oxygen and hopelessly damaged. Mowamba's body grew in a normal way, but his mind was frozen in time. This child cried frequently and seemed to suffer severe frustration. He would clench his little fists and appeared to tense every muscle in his frail body. At these times we gently pried open his hands, one finger at a time, and massaged each one. Sometimes we would rub his back and work his bony arms and legs at the elbows and knees in an effort to help him relax. Oftentimes I just sat on a floor mat and held him in my arms. When he looked up at me, his big brown eyes brimming with tears, it broke my heart for all I could do for him was hold him closer and love him more.

Had Angela been born in the fourteenth century, she could well have been a model for the "divine" Raphael's coy, endearing cherubs had it not been for one thing. Her eyes were filled with terror and bewilderment. It would have been a blessing if she had no memory, but she could recall bedtime stories, brothers and sisters, picnics, birthday cakes, loving parents — all that make childhood such a magical time. But these things were gone now. The disease that ravaged her body had now afforded her a lifetime's measure of pain and loss in five short years. She had periods of intense suffering, and her debilitation had advanced to the point that she could neither speak nor walk. When she began to scream, was it the agony of her physical pain? Or was she wondering what she could have possibly done to merit such punishment? I wanted so to take her in my arms and comfort her, but I must not. We had been instructed not to react sympathetically to her outbursts, for she could become a spoiled demanding *infant terrible*. She must learn to deal with the life that was now hers and forget what had been.

Another well-remembered child is fourteen-year-old Luther. Like Peter Pan he would never grow up. Some accident of fate had stranded him in infancy, in both mind and body. Luther did not belong in Schoolroom C., but we all knew him for he was such a little gadabout. The volunteers loved to take him around to visit the various schoolrooms. No wheelchair could accommodate his tiny size, but he did have his very own personal conveyance, a sort of double-wide skateboard. The top surface had velvety-soft carpeting and a strap to hold him securely, as well as a cord for pulling this contraption across the floor. We all loved towing him around like some mechanical pull toy while he giggled and waved his miniature arms and legs. Perhaps he experienced peace because his body and mind were in sync, something Mowamba and Angela were unable to feel.

Twelve-year-old John was unique in several ways. Unlike any other child in the home, he had normal mental faculties; and he was the only one to die during my tenure. Though wheelchair-bound, John liked to visit around and often came to Schoolroom C. I never did know what the medical doctors called his illness, but we all knew this child belonged to death, and death would claim its own erelong. When John became so ill he had to be taken to the hospital, some of us gathered in the hall to wish him Godspeed as he was wheeled on a gurney to the waiting ambulance. As he passed by he said, "I'll run in heaven." In three days he was dead.

Mara was very special to me. While every child in the home touched my heart, Mara touched my soul as well. She was born deaf, blind, and severely mentally deficient. I think she must have been very special to the workers in the dormitory wing also, for she came to *school* each day in a pretty dress with the clean scent of soap about her, her long brown hair braided in two pigtails and tied with brightly colored bows. Her arms and legs dangled uselessly like those of a rag doll, but they were always adoringly adorned. She wore t-strap sandals like the ones I had worn as a child, and her anklets were frilly with ruffles and lace. Her tiny fingernails were often polished to a rosy luster, and sometimes she wore her Mickey Mouse watch.

Fortunately Mara could eat, and I believe it must have been

her one pleasure in life. She accepted each spoonful of pureed food eagerly and seemed to savor each one. Yet, when it was gone she never complained and was a paragon of patience. In the two years I served in the Home, I never heard her cry or even whimper — only an occasional long weary sigh. Mara grew a bit chubby, no doubt due to her robust appetite. Eventually I found it difficult to lift her. I never did know her age but experienced surprise the first time I changed her diaper and saw pubic hair.

And then there was Barry, who had a metal rod in his back to prevent his slumping over and damaging his vital organs; and little David whose facial features had been skewed in the womb. But he could feed himself if you could abide the mess, and he could stand in the corner unaided as long as a minute with his leg braces and loving arms nearby to catch him if his body flagged — his spirit never did. And a boy named Christopher, affectionately called Critter, whom I spoiled shamelessly because he had the sweetest face and longest eye lashes I had ever seen.

Where are they now? I often wonder. I know they are no longer at the Linnville Children's Home for they are no longer children. Others have come to take their places. But, wherever they are, it is my earnest prayer that one day they may run in heaven — all of them. And may they run, and skip, and play leapfrog, and catch fireflies. And may they turn the handle of the jack-in-the-box all by themselves, then shout with glee when the funny little man in the red-peaked hat with his big hook nose pops out. After that, and only after that, may they rest eternally in peace.

More Than Meets the Eye

Carolyn Lineberry

Usually I prefer not to emphasize physical characteristics, but I find it fascinating that Carolyn Lineberry is a fair-skinned, blue-eyed blond of English and Irish descent (with a dash from Alsace), teaching at a public school of primarily Arab students and administration in Dearborn, Michigan. She is learning about the struggles and successes of the people from Jordan, Syria, Lebanon, Iran, Iraq, and other Middle Eastern countries who have settled in this area for decades. As she learns, Carolyn is teaching children and their parents about America, our ideals and what we stand for. Seeking understanding and always finding humor in this cultural exchange, she is, in her own way, changing the world.

When I was a child I used to dream about growing up and doing something extraordinary. Usually, the dream involved being a beautiful and famous singer. Playing the radio or a record and using my hairbrush as a microphone, I would watch myself in the mirror, imagining adoring fans cheering me on. As I grew older reality set in, along with the realization that I was never going to be a famous singer.

So, it was time to think about a more realistic career. I still wanted to do something important—something that would make a difference in other people's lives. Growing up in the middle of a large family, I often helped my mother care for my younger siblings. I began to think about becoming a pediatrician since I enjoyed being with children and was drawn to the ideals of being a doctor. Well, learning of the many years of schooling required to achieve that goal, as well as the emotional difficulties involved in caring for sick children, soon changed my mind again! During senior year of high school I made the decision to become an elementary school teacher. One interesting and challenging journey ended and another began.

Due to finances and changing schools it took me a long time to finish college, but I finally graduated in 1990 with a degree in Elementary Education. By then I was married and living in Dearborn, Michigan. I began my career with two years of substitute teaching in the local school district. The East end of the city was becoming populated with many families of Arab descent. The schools were filled with children whose first language was Arabic. Teaching in Dearborn was going to be even more challenging with English as a second language for so many students!

The following year I was hired to teach first grade. I was excited, but also very nervous. That first year was quite challenging, and I felt overwhelmed with responsibility. There were over twenty children under my tutelage each day. In addition to teaching, there were lessons to plan for several different subjects, classroom management plans to write, guided reading groups (based on reading level) to organize, materials checklists, and grading and student assessments to be completed. It was also important to serve as a role model and set a good example for these youngsters.

During my first year I sometimes wondered if I could do it all. It was arduous and yet enjoyable work. I stuck with it, and as the years went by it got easier—not because the work got easier —rather because I was more experienced. Experience *is* the best teacher, and I was becoming more comfortable as well as more capable in my role.

The children who attend my school are also from a lower income bracket. Their socioeconomic class and their language limits contribute greatly to the learning challenges they face. My students all speak English as well as Arabic. Most of the parents do as well, but (probably more than) a few of them struggle with the English language, and this makes it very difficult for them to help their child with homework. There is a bilingual classroom for each grade. Students who have been in the U.S. for less than a year and others who struggle with English are placed in these classrooms. We also have bilingual paraprofessionals to assist the teachers with teaching reading groups and to translate when needed.

Parent-Teacher Conferences are held each fall. During the conference the parent and teacher discuss academic concerns, student conduct, the teacher's classroom expectations, homework guidelines, and any concerns the parent may have. These conferences are also an opportunity to gain insight into the family situation and learn more about the child. Sometimes I find that a family is going through a divorce or a child is being bullied, and I had no idea that these events were taking place.

Discussing these issues enables me to increase my awareness, be more understanding, and perhaps approach a situation created by cultural diversity in a different manner.

The conference is also an opportunity to suggest ways in which the parents can help their child at home in order to achieve more at school. This means making sure the child is eating properly, getting his or her homework done, following rules at home, and getting enough sleep each night. When children have consistency at home as well as at school, they tend to have a better understanding and appreciation of what is expected of them. Parental support is very important in this process, and it is imperative that students understand how parents and teachers are working together for their success.

I wish I could say I have the support of every parent each year, but I don't. Some of them think it is enough to simply ask their child if he has any homework. However, more follow-up is required to be certain that assignments are understood, completed properly, placed back into the child's backpack, and returned to school on time.

Over the years I have discovered that many of the parents do not take an active interest in their child's schooling. This is true in regard to behavioral issues as well. In the Arabic culture, males are not disciplined as much as females. It is considered an honor for a father to have a son. A son can carry on the family name; and oftentimes if a family owns a store or a gas station, the son is expected to be a part of the business when he is older. The males in the family appear to be more respected, while the females are expected to cook, clean, and care for the children. Because males are viewed as the more domineering and respected gender, I sometimes do not get the necessary parental support when it comes to behavioral problems. This is especially true of some of the fathers, who do not take what I say seriously and make excuses for their sons. Lack of discipline at home combined with cultural disrespect for women can create a real *disconnect* from my efforts to correct and guide male students in the classroom.

I once had an experience in which a father felt that I was being too hard on his son, and he didn't like it. He complained, defended, and basically refused to take any action. However, I was continually guiding the boy's conduct and helping him with ways to improve his studies. When positive changes became apparent in the son's actions and academic achievement, the father's attitude changed, too. At the next conference Dad was the epitome of graciousness, singing my praises and bemoaning the fact that I would not be teaching his son the following year as well!

Now in my fourteenth year as a teacher, I am presently teaching second grade. My students have a variety of personalities and varying degrees of academic capabilities. Teachers today have many other roles, including counselor, nutritionist, caregiver, and nurturer. Some children have a lot of emotional baggage and need help working through these issues.

Just recently I had a positive experience with an emotionally troubled student. He had been acting out and required disciplinary action for various reasons throughout the school year. Nothing seemed to be working to change his behavior. The mother and I spoke, and I explained that I would like to try a little reverse psychology with her son, hoping the approach would be more effective than stronger disciplinary action. She agreed.

Lavatory time was a particular problem and became the first order of business. The student had been throwing large quantities of paper into the toilet, purposely clogging it and making a terrible mess. He was given the job of Bathroom Captain. His mission was to watch the other boys in our class during the bathroom break and report to me if anyone was breaking any rules. He was very proud of his job and the trust I was showing toward him. He performed well that day and no damage was suffered under his careful watch. Encouraged by this, I assigned him the task for the entire week. The boy was excited about his new responsibilities, and his resultant behavior the best it had ever been.

Meanwhile, Friday was coming — time for the coveted "Star Student of the Week" award. It had previously been doubtful that my little Bathroom Captain would ever be a recipient. However, I decided to honor him with the award on the Friday he finished his tour of washroom duty, uncertain there would come a time when he would warrant it again! The class sat quietly on the floor, facing the *Star Student* bulletin board. I announced the student's name and my reasons for choosing him. His photo was placed on the board along with some stars he had filled out about himself. *(Why is he proud of himself? What is his favorite thing about school? What are his goals for the future?)* All of the children applauded enthusiastically. Then I turned to him and asked, "How does this make you feel?"

"I feel GREAT!!" was the reply. He had a big smile on his face, and at that moment I truly felt I had made a difference in this boy's life. A child who has been constantly told he is doing wrong, and has been punished on numerous occasions for misbehaving, was finally being recognized and rewarded for doing something good. It was a wonderful feeling—for both of us.

Another unexpected event demonstrated how little things can mean a lot, especially to the goslings under my wing. In teaching students about good nutrition and the importance of healthy eating, they are asked to bring something for morning snack-time. A note is sent home at the beginning of the school year, emphasizing this lesson and listing acceptable foods the child may bring to school. One of the girls never brought a snack. Continually providing something from my emergency stash, I would follow up with a reminder to bring something from home. When pressed, the child explained that she had nothing to bring from home; her father could not afford to buy anything so frivolous as *snack foods*. Doomed to digging into my meager supply of pretzels and crackers for the duration, I wondered how many other children I would be providing for by the end of the school year.

To my surprise, when class resumed after our mid-winter break in February, I found we had received a state grant that would provide every child in kindergarten through fifth grade with a daily fruit or vegetable snack! This took a load off my mind and spelled relief for many of the families as well. It's funny how things have a way of working out sometimes, and the joy to be found in small rewards.

Another school year will shortly be coming to an end. I will take what I learned from these experiences and use them to become a better and more effective teacher when I return in the fall. Each new class brings new challenges. My goal is to continue to be a role model and guide my students to make the best choices and be the best they can be during the time we share together. My hope is that they will take what they learn from me and carry it with them, not only to the next school year, but throughout their lives.

The Accidental Tour Guide

Charlotte Claar

Charlotte Claar lived in Illinois among the ivied halls of academia for many years and holds two degrees from the University of Illinois. I met her when I moved to Vero Beach and she was already a veteran of the creative writing group I had joined. She is an interesting person, a fine friend, and a wise woman. She is an excellent editor and one of the best writers I know, certainly a personal favorite. The following is one of her many travel adventures.

Those persons who provide promotional material for the travel industry have a proclivity for hyperbole. With their wide-angle lenses and their wild-angle prose they make an ordinary hotel room look like the sultan's quarters in the Pink Palace of Poobah. We're talking hype here, five-star hype.

My husband, Jack, and I were just going out the door of Trafalgar Travel in the arcade of our London hotel when the agent we had been consulting called to us. She hurried over and handed Jack yet another brochure and said, "This could be just the weekend package to Paris you are looking for." He stuffed it into his bulging briefcase.

Back in our hotel room, Jack dumped the contents of his briefcase onto the bed. Among the more interesting items of fallout were one London-Rome round trip airline ticket, a petrified peanut butter and jelly sandwich, a dirty sock, and a passel of Paris brochures.

The ticket, sock, and sandwich were Jack's. We were in Europe that summer while he was on sabbatical leave from the University of Illinois, and he had agreed to attend a conference on world hunger in Rome. As for the sock, he muttered something that sounded like Pee-U and dropped it into the wastebasket. The sandwich received more attention because before he dispatched it to the garbage, he muttered "If I'd known it was in my briefcase I would have eaten it on the trip over instead of that no-fat, no-salt, no-taste special airline glop you ordered for me."

The travel brochures were mine. My sisters, Ellie and Addie, were arriving in a few days for a visit; and we had decided the three of us should go to Paris for the weekend while Jack was in Rome. This European adventure was a heart-thumper for my sisters as neither had been out of the United States. It was important we find just the right Parisian experience.

Jack pawed through the pile of brochures, chose one, scanned it, and began to laugh. "Listen to this! Come to spectacular Paris and stay in our *selected* (not to be confused with *select*) hotel, the magnificent Grand Palace, where you just may have a room with a view of the elegant sculptured flower beds of the Tuileries Gardens." (Yes, if you hang by your heels from the window ledge and it isn't washday at the Chinese laundry across the street!)

I found a goodie and extorted Jack to listen to mine. "Ladies, come to the Paris of your dreams and have a romantic encounter with a French Adonis in a beret." (What it really means is, you may be pinched on the bottom by a myopic masher in a feed store cap.) I thought it was hilarious. Jack yawned.

My husband had to rebut and searched through the pile of pamphlets until he found one he liked. "Take the elevator to the top of the Eiffel Tower. Step out onto the uppermost stage and feast your eyes on a breathtaking bird's eye view of the Parisian panorama." (Yes, but don't look up with your mouth open or your feast could come from the other end of the bird.) My reaction was *yuck.* Jack thought it was a riot.

"My turn! Now hear this. Visit the incomparable Louvre and smile back at that enigmatic lady, the Mona Lisa." (But try to forget that spoilsport of a dentist who just had to go and tell us the lady smiles funny because she has bad teeth.)

Jack likes to have the last word. This game wasn't over yet. He studied another brochure, chuckled and read, "Dally over a sparkling aperitif at a charming sidewalk cafe." (Yes, but before you do, better stop by a war surplus store and buy a gas mask if you enjoy the beneficial effects of oxygen.)

The contest of one-upmanship ended when I found the perfect package. Time to get serious. This weekend package included round trip airfare, a well-located hotel for two nights, breakfasts, a bus sightseeing tour of Paris, and a gala dinner in a fine restaurant Saturday night. All within our budget. Perfect!

After seeing Jack off for Rome, the three sisters headed for our Paris weekend. The trip across the channel was brief. Our pilot had barely tucked the wheels into the plane's belly when they came rumbling down again as we began our descent into Charles De Gaulle Airport.

Our group was met by the tour guide and we piled into a bus. All were in a holiday mood as we sang endless verses of "Frère Jacques." We clapped and cheered mightily as our driver maneuvered through those narrow cobblestone alleyways. A congenial group! We were in for a weekend of fun.

When our driver pulled up to a hotel I reached for my luggage. But that wasn't the way it worked. The guide read off several names. These people grabbed their bags and followed him into the hotel. He returned in a few minutes and we drove on. This routine continued a dozen times with one difference. I no longer reached for my luggage. We were the last ones on the bus when the guide led us into our hotel. He saw that we were registered, handed me an envelope and said, "Here are your chits for the bus tour and dinner. Have a grand weekend. I'll be back for you Sunday afternoon around five."

I now knew my growing fear was fact. This was a package tour all right, but not a *guided* package as I had assumed. My heart sank into the soles of my sensible shoes. There were my trusting sisters looking at me with starry eyes. They didn't know I had always been with Jack. He was the consummate traveler and took care of everything. He had mastered the art of backing off little old ladies in tennis shoes who tried to push ahead of him in airport lines. He employed a deft maneuver involving an elbow synchronized with a knee bend and a size fourteen E shoe that sent the old girl scurrying to her rightful place at the end of the line. And Jack could have a sniffy sneery waiter muttering to himself and looking down nervously to see whether his fly was open, his boutonniere dangling, or he'd forgotten to wear socks.

But one of the most dramatic moments in the annals of travel occurred in Rome where I actually saw Jack pick up a pint-sized pickpocket who had just lifted his wallet, turn the kid upside down and shake him by the heels until his billfold fell out —along with several others.

However, most impressive of all, Jack could say, "Where's the toilet?" in six languages and one international gesture.

As for me, in no foreign country had I ever hailed a cab, exchanged currency, purchased a ticket, registered in a hotel, or tipped a waiter. But my sisters didn't know that, and I wasn't about to tell them.

Fortunately our hotel was well located and we could walk to the most important tourist spots. Also, we were picked up and returned to our hotel on the included sightseeing tour. My big worry was the gala dinner. The chits were for a place in Montmartre, miles across the city. My inclination was to simply forego this meal and find a restaurant nearby. But I knew this dinner was a big part of the package cost, and I just couldn't do that to my sisters. We could take a taxi, but that would compromise the community coffer. There was always the metro, but the idea of herding our little band of pilgrims across Paris at night scared me a lot. However, after listening to our concierge's reassuring words, we decided to risk the metro.

That evening we walked to the subway station and spent half an hour studying the system and watching others. On the wall was a large map of Paris with the routes and stations marked. A flashing light identified our location, and when you pressed the button that indicated your destination, another light came on there and the route between lit up, with flashing lights indicating where one must change trains. Eventually we decided we understood the system. I walked to the ticket window, put down my francs, and requested in my very best high school French, "Trwa belay ah Momar, seel vu pleh." The kind lady showed a great deal of composure when she didn't snicker.

After distributing the tickets we passed confidently through the turnstile, each placing her ticket in the slot and then withdrawing it. We walked through a heavy door that closed behind us and found ourselves in another large room. I studied the situation and noticed another door with "la sortie" written above it. "All right, girls, this is an exit to the trains." So we went through that door and it clanged shut. Still, where were the trains? Then I noticed the room seemed oddly familiar. We were back in the lobby again! The door we had passed through was an exit all right—an exit for *arriving* trains. But, all was not lost; we could recover. We still had our tickets. We could go through the turnstile again, and this time I would find *la entre* door. I stepped confidently up to the turnstile and placed my ticket in the slot, but a bell began to ring and a red light flashed, and I fully expected to see the lobby swarming with gendarmes any second. Some sneaky type was trying to use an invalid ticket. "Let's get out of here!" was my urgent command. And we moved!

Hurrying back to the hotel, we had the bellman negotiate for a taxi and rode in style to our gala dinner. We dined at the Mère Catherine Restaurant in an historic house dating to 1793. It was charming—not all froufrou or gilded Louis the Fourteenth, but friendly Country French where three awe-stricken insecure tourists could enjoy a superb meal and feel comfortable. How unfortunate it would have been if my timidity had prevented our having this delightful experience.

When dinner was over, I approached the cashier about calling a cab for us. She explained this was not the custom. We should stand on the steps of Sacre Coeur Cathedral, for taxis came by every few minutes.

We did as suggested but waited what seemed like an eternity. I knew my cab hailing skill lacked decisiveness. So, as midnight approached I became more aggressive and was most heartened when a taxi finally stopped.

Our hotel was a very welcome sight. I decided to be a generous tipper but realized later I had been more than generous. Numbers are not my best thing, and because of conversion problems I had given the driver a tip of francs equivalent to about thirty dollars. And, at that time, that was almost enough to buy a seat on the New York Stock Exchange. But I was so relieved the evening had been very pleasant, except for the faux pas that could have landed us in the Bastille, I decided not to let it ruin our day. Besides, Paris is la la land, and it was only funny money anyway.

Did Addie and Ellie ever know how reluctant I had been to be an accidental tour guide? I hope not. If they did, they were too kind to say anything, and I saw no point in telling them. I simply slipped extra francs the equivalent of thirty dollars into the kitty—or, was it a hundred? Whatever, it was worth it.

The Brightness of Being

Christina M. Fratcher

As if by magic, I discovered the Dragonfly Quilt Shop the first week it opened, on a quiet street behind the police station. Others were also drawn by the carefully placed signs, the colorful building, the flowers, and the young, spirited, Italian-American owner, Christina Fratcher. Her long dark hair swept up in a pony tail, she is ready to work on her labor of love, whether it is ordering fabric, organizing a website, offering classes, or greeting customers. (Not to mention painting the exterior building purple, stenciling interior walls, arguing with City inspectors, and cleaning.) There is always soap in the bathroom. Ask her advice on fabric choice and she will say, "You know me, the brighter the better." Christina asked if she could write in the style of a letter to me, in the rambling rose manner in which she speaks. I agreed.

How do you find your destiny? You know that *journey* people are always talking about, the road taken or not taken, the twists and turns along the way? Well, my destiny involves being a volunteer Girl Scout troop leader, a family member's fatal illness, and a somewhat disappointing career — all serendipitous as it turned out, because they conspired together to lead me to a place where I love being today.

I don't know if I ever told you that I used to be a Girl Scout leader. I put Blake, my daughter, in GS because it was really all I could afford at the time, and I knew it would offer her a way to have some worthwhile experiences and make friends. I didn't like her leader; she struck me as mean-spirited and no fun at all. I thought, *I can do this and oh, so much better.* So I did and certainly was much better.

We had some wonderful times. One of our favorites was a trip to Savannah. We were able to stay in a small museum. Oh, no, not just any museum. (Roaming art galleries at midnight or telling scary stories amongst the mummies was not to be our lot.) This was the Girl Scout First Headquarters, bequeathed to the Girl Scouts by Juliette Gordon Low, the founder of the organization. The girls had a ball! They were so funny, walking all over in their underwear and brushing their teeth right in the middle of the lecture room. They had the whole place to themselves for one night. It was great fun. They went on Ghost Walk tours — and Savannah has plenty of ghosts. We also took a horse and buggy ride and saw a bunch of the historic Squares.

During my six years as a troop leader, I took the girls horseback riding and on many other outings. We went to see plays. We worked on craft projects and had a lot of laughs. At the time, my daughter was not thrilled about having to be in the same troop as her mom — how uncool. But now that she's grown, she talks about all the stuff she did and how great it was. I see the other girls now and then and they have such good memories about it.

However, Scouting is more than play. There is (albeit fun) work to be done. One of the badges the girls wanted to earn was a sewing badge. I, unlike some of the leaders, really made them earn their badges; I mean really *earn* them. So I met this woman named Joann who was a quilter and a fabulous sewer. I don't even remember how I met her, but she lived in a log cabin house in the woods. Really *Little House on the Prairie* type, but larger. She had a quilt shop her husband had built on the side of the house. It was pretty big, with a separate entrance overlooking the most beautiful wooded landscape. Looking out the windows — they spanned an entire wall of the shop — was like being out in the wilderness. You get the picture.

At the time I was working with the girls on their sewing badges, my mother was diagnosed with lung cancer. She was dying and it was all very sudden, with no real time to mourn. During her illness, I often took some of the girls in my troop to meet some of the other ladies who did sewing and quilting together. It was so nice; they would have potlucks and just be laughing and enjoying each others' company. Now, I was a great deal younger than all of them, perhaps 33 or 34, but I wanted to join their group. So I did. It was therapy for me; it took my mind off of what was actually going on with my mother.

All my life I sewed or made "crafty" things, or at least *I* thought they were crafty. We lived in Ohio when I was younger, on five acres of land with a pond and woods all around. As a girl I would go deep into the woods and cut down vines and make things out of them. I would take leaves and press them in my mother's wax paper and tell her they were placemats. Once I actually picked all the grapes we had growing on the side of our house and made — what I told my mother was — wine. I followed the directions on something; and again, who knows where I was getting my information. I left it in a cool place in our basement and after a few months asked my mom and her friends to try it. *Oh*, they said, *it was delicious*. I think they threw it away when I was out of sight. So you see, I didn't just decide to start quilting, it was a pattern of events.

My mother was eventually placed on a respirator, and I was still showing up to finish that quilt. I would sit next to Joann and sew and cry and sew and cry some more. She would talk to me very supportively about my mom. I was my mother's Power of Attorney (POA) and I just could not at that moment take her off the respirator. Now let me back up — my mother had only found out three weeks before that she had cancer. Her situation was deteriorating rapidly. The doctor said, and I quote, she "had never seen lungs that bad on someone who was still living." She was only 52! The year was 1998, and sometimes I cannot believe it was so long ago because it seems like only yesterday.

My quilt, unfinished, was left and forgotten at Joann's for years. She herself had things going on, and her husband was in a horrible car accident, so I was not able to finish the quilt for some time. When I did get it several years later, it had faded from exposure to the sun somewhere in her shop. I took it and added a plain backing, which, let me add, I would never do now, but I did, and then I quilted it. Now it is really ugly and I cannot believe I made it with *those* colors, but again, at the time those were the only quilting fabrics available. But that quilt has great sentimental value. Today it hangs on the back of a sofa in my home, where no one is allowed to touch it; still faded but my daughter's favorite because it represents her grandmother with whom she was very close.

Finishing that quilt after such a long time sparked my desire to continue quilting. I went to the only quilt shop in town at the time. I made friends, laughed, gossiped—yes, I gossip. I started tossing up the idea of owning my own quilt shop. This was further motivated by the quilt shop I went to. It was not the cleanest and it never had soap in the bathrooms. I found only mediocre fabrics and no great notions from which to learn new quilting skills. I would often sit and sew and say to anyone who would listen at my table, "If I owned a quilt shop...I would not have animals present...I would have soap in the bathrooms...I would have a wide selection of books and patterns and classes, etc."

By this time I was a registered nurse and had worked several different positions trying to find my niche in nursing. I worked in orthopedics, mental health, diabetes, oncology (which was my favorite), endoscopy, and it goes on, but at that time I was working on what is referred to as "per diem." It really should be called an "if we need you or not" position because I was getting called in here and there; I was getting called in more and more. I could have gone full-time, but the hospital I work at does not, and I repeat does *not*, pay their nurses a competitive rate. Yes, I could have looked elsewhere, but that old saying "the devil you know is better than the devil you don't know" kept me in check.

I made up my mind after several years that I was going to open a quilt shop. I didn't know how or with what money, but I was going to do it, and I *did!* It has been a fabulous experience, and all the people I have met have turned out to be truly rewarding friends. I have been lucky to have such loyal supporters among my customers. Though I am not rolling in the money and I still cannot afford to hire an employee (though several volunteer), it has all been good. We recently moved to a new location that is larger and definitely better in so many ways. Each time the customers come in they see something different we have done. Last week we put up french doors for better lighting and they look great. We are a work in progress.

I really do not have any one thing to credit for my quilting or being a nurse, no particular friend; it is all those places we hit on our journey. All those little stops along the way, some side roads, some dead ends, and some yard sales. Yes, yard sales, with great sales and things we have spent too much on and maybe we would not have bought it if we had to do it over again. Or maybe the price was high—but worth every penny. In my case, a Girl Scout troop, my mother's tragic illness and death, struggles and rewards in my nursing career, the friends who boosted me up, and my quirky dream to open a quilt shop led me toward a destiny in unexpected places. But I ended up just where I was meant to be.

The E-Mail Exchange
Cindy Meier, FNP-BC

Cindy Meier is still a new friend and therefore somewhat of a mystery to me. I know she and her husband took an old parcel of Florida grove land and together turned it into a fabulous home and a spacious workshop, with a pond, a pool and spa, an orchid house, stone pathways, flowering trees, and a big vegetable garden. Two cocker spaniels have the run of the place. The house is interesting, large, and built on a round plan with bay windows, both cozy and spacious rooms, and lots of light. Curiously, it is located just down the road from the chimpanzee sanctuary in Fort Pierce, and Cindy can often catch the howls and shrieks of monkey shenanigans on the prevailing winds. Cindy uses the initials FNP-BC after her name, which means she is a Family Nurse Practitioner-Board Certified. Her work takes her into the homes of the elderly. The medical care provided is traditional, but incorporates holistic methods; she loves to listen to her patients and they have many stories to tell. She is from a family of nine children, and they all seem to turn to her for solace, comfort, financial aid, temporary housing, health solutions, a good meal, and a listening ear. To Cindy, there is nothing like a cruise with her husband, Gary, for relaxation and escape, and they have enjoyed them all over the world. This year she added the delight of a grandchild, who unfortunately lives some distance away, in Oregon. I thought it might be interesting to show her busy but fulfilling life in the form of an e-mail exchange between her and me. It begins and ends with Thanks. Perhaps that is why she is so blessed.

November 2009
Cynthia Hurst: Looking forward to Thanksgiving at your place. What time?

Cindy Meier: Plan to have meal around 2-3 (late lunch/early dinner). Come anytime before that. We'll visit. See you then.

CH: What shall we bring?

CM: Don't bring anything...you could bring some wine.

CH: Had a great time. Your house is fantastic! And the doggies are so cute. And the orchid house you built—amazing. (Hard to believe what you can do with a few acres of old Florida grove land.)

CM: With months of planning, building, rock piles, digging holes, planting, tending, cleaning, and mowing, this too can be yours! Thank goodness for the golf cart and the pool.

CH: And wine.

January 2010
CM: Thank you so much for considering me for the Diamond Project. I will review your letter. I am excited about your endeavors. I strive to do my writing in addition to all my professional responsibilities. Thanks again.

February 2010

CM: Planning on submitting writing for your Diamond Project. I plan to get it in the mail by the weekend. Hopefully will be to you by Monday Feb 8. Please be looking for it. Is Feb 8 concrete deadline? Thanks.

CH: You've got plenty of time. I haven't even sent out an official deadline yet. Probably end of April. Everyone's so busy...

CM: Thank you for clarification. I will definitely participate. Let me know schedule and count me as a Yes.

CM: Thanks for additional info. Let me know when you can have tea, lunch, wine or whatever.

CH: Let's have lunch to discuss. Or tea or coffee. Can't do wine in the afternoon unless I'm in France and everyone naps afterward.

CM: Would love it. My brother from Alaska just got back from 3 months in Thailand and coming here the 15th. My daughter here first week of March. We leave March 26 for 14-day cruise. But would really like to meet up. Any time—I can squeeze it in when things slow down for you.

CH: Week of March 1st is good, any day. (Wed I have something at noon, but later would be OK.) Let me know. I can drive out to your place or you can come here!

CM: Damn. My daughter here from Feb 27 to March 7. We are going to St. Augustine for a few days. Can we do it next week after that?

CH: Sure, just call any time.

CM: Could you give me contact number again?

CH: Here are my numbers (but cell is not on unless I'm out)

CM: Can you do lunch March 17 or tea/coffee?

CH: Wednesday is the only day I have a set appt (French group). It's usually 12-2, so I could meet for coffee around 3. Your house? I'm happy to drive out there. Let me know. The rest of the week I can meet any time. Let's figure something out.

March 2010
CM: How about Thursday? Difficult for me to say what time I would be done in a day. If I am in Vero, I can stop and do what I need to do. How about Thursday 3 pm at Starbucks?

CM: Good to see you. Loved the visit. Book I mentioned with publisher is called "This is not the Life I Ordered." Check it out. Have other books in like interests. Will check publishers. I would really like to write about stories from my elderly patients. Talk to you soon.

CH: Good to talk about your ideas. Can't deal with the caffeine shakes but I love the Chi Tea Lattes anyway!! Have to meet at McDonald's for a mocha frappe sometime. Delicious! (Employee told me they have calories "you can never get rid of.") Worth every one! And no caffeine shakes...

CM: It's the whipped cream.

CH: Subject: Courage
This is just a boost to encourage you in your writing. I know I said "no excuses" necessary but this is about people who said yes and are now bowing out. Or the ones I haven't heard from. Everyone is busy. I chose you for a reason. Your contribution is important. Don't lose heart. Consider this "gentle pressure" of the good kind.

CM: Thanks for the Courage pep talk. I will be working on my submission over the cruise and send to you when I return. You have some good resources for publication. Another book I liked is "I will Not Die an Unlived Life." Good luck. Will be in touch. Cindy

CH: I'm sure you'll be working hard writing for my book while ON A CRUISE. Ha! Looking for a publisher but need manuscript and table of contents. I'm still at gentle nudge stage. Have a Mai Tai for me.

CM: Awesome. So glad you're starting the great search for a publisher. Starbucks date fun. We will get together when I am back if you have time before you travel. Looking forward to relaxing.

CH: Thanks Cindy. Of course I already knew I could count on you. Checked out the publisher you recommended today. It sounds perfect. When I have more material collected I will send them a proposal. Happy cruising!!
Cynthia
P.S. I really enjoyed our Starbucks "date" too.

April 2010
CM: Having slow progress on submission.

CH: Do not be afraid.

CM: Just a bit overwhelming and humbling.

CM: Apologize I couldn't get it together to submit writing for your book. Too much on my plate. Behind in too many things. Going this next week to Oregon to see grandbaby, Cora. I am sure your book will be a hit. Stay in touch and let's have lunch from time to time.

CH: Cindy, I am so happy for you and grandbaby. Have a wonderful time.
Would you give me permission to write something about you? This is with the understanding that you would read and approve before publication. I would really like to write about the home you and Gary have made in Florida —It's so unusual, a side of Florida most people don't see. And your work also. And our (still forming) friendship.
Let me know. Cynthia

CM: You are too generous. If you want, sure, go ahead and write something. Send me your version and I'll look it over. Thanks.

May 2010
CM: Are you free for lunch soon? I have a gift certificate for Ocean Grill. How about Tue, Thu or Fri next week?

We didn't meet for several months. Cindy and Gary were reorganizing their lives and reducing their work schedules; they went on a cruise, and spent some time in Oregon with family. I was also traveling, spending time at our home in North Carolina, entertaining guests from France, and visiting family and friends in Pennsylvania where my husband is from. Cindy and I finally met for lunch at Mojo's in Vero Beach in July 2010.

July 2010

CH: I can't believe a tuna sandwich on whole grain toast could be that good. Maybe it was the salad with honey mustard dressing. And we both ordered exactly the same thing. And the iced tea was excellent.

CM: Maybe it was the funny waitress or the good company, or just the atmosphere of Mojo's. I promise I will get busy and give you some extra details for the book soon. We're looking for property in the Northwest, both working three days a week; I'm finishing my children's book, getting back into painting pictures again, and the usual stuff around the house. Other than that I'm totally free!

CH: Summer is melting away from us! Just give me incidents, cruise places, house and garden bits, work stories. I can fill in the rest.

CM: Going on another Caribbean cruise in November.

CH: Well, that brings us full-circle to November again!

CM: What are you doing for Thanksgiving?

The Art of Reinventing Yourself
Devin Reed

Devin Reed is a banker by profession, a mother by preference, a musician by way of the past and – presently learning to research and develop patents – an inventor in the making. She is the picture of kind and caring, smart and perceptive. Her appeal lies in a dewy freshness with an underlying air of competence. Devin possesses the dichotomy of being traditional yet anything but conventional. Blessed with attractive looks, ability and luck, she follows the path that calls to her. This mode of traveling through life has led her to some pretty interesting places. In the process, she has discovered the art of continually reinventing herself.

When you walk into the bank where I work as a financial officer and see the petite blond in the glass-walled office on your way to the teller window, you may think *what is this kid doing here?* Yes, there are times when I have had to work against the dumb-blond image; and years of will-to-succeed and well-honed competence are the only ways of dealing with the problem—and the asset— of youth. Being able to reinvent yourself doesn't hurt either.

Dreams, ability, work, opportunity, luck and timing are the tools for success, whether you aspire to be a good student, tradesman, entrepreneur, professional, or work in the performing arts. Along the way I ended up as almost all of them! Part of being young is trying different things that interest you. It's the only way to find your calling. Faith in God also helped and bestowed many blessings upon my efforts.

There's a story about a man who arrives at the Pearly Gates upon his death. The Lord tells the man that, having led a good life, he is to be gained entrance into heaven. The man is happy to hear this news, of course, but has only one question. "God, I did my best to be your humble and faithful servant on earth, to be a good family man and friend, to work hard and to serve the less fortunate; but I was mediocre at most things. You never blessed me with a great talent. Why is that?"

The response came quickly. "My son, I made you the greatest pianist the world had ever known. But you never tried to play the piano."

In reality, this person would probably have been drawn to play the piano at some point in his life, but the lesson remains clear. We have to try many things and respond to whatever we are drawn to in order to best utilize our gifts.

In my case the talent search began in the entertainment industry, with which I was heavily involved throughout middle and high school. By the time I graduated, I had done several print media jobs (photo shoots) along with commercials. For five years I had a singing contract with an independent label, and trained at Transcontinental Studios in Orlando, Florida. It was there that I met some of the big names of the time — particularly the popular boy bands NSYNC and the Backstreet Boys. But I also worked with Mandy Moore, Gloria Estefan, Kevin Bacon and others.

Today, with computers and advanced technology, many aspiring singers and other artists put something together and promote themselves. But when I was in the business everything revolved around agents, contracts, making deals and climbing the ladder of success. Few people realize the many layers to the entertainment industry. Few acts are an instant success. Most start on their first rung to the top with auditions, auto shows, cruise ships, theme parks and resorts. My venues were places like Hard Rock Live, SeaWorld, Wet N Wild, Panther Stadium, and Swig. I loved every minute of the music industry, from the writing process to performing on stage. It was a great rush!

The only thing that put a halt to my music career was the fact that the record label owner married and moved to Africa. Unfortunately, he had not released me from my contract, so no other label was able to pick me up for at least three more years. Like everyone else, I had financial obligations to meet and was forced to look elsewhere for work. Perhaps I will return to music one day, but at the time it just felt like a bad experience, and a break from the industry was warranted.

Well, not a *total* break—this was, after all, what I knew and loved. Shortly following high school graduation I happened to be at an audition and met a project manager for BMW. Offered a job in Los Angeles for a month to be a spokesperson at the LA Auto Show, I gladly accepted. It was a terrific and fun experience that came with the additional offer of the opportunity to travel for their season.

However, I was looking for a *real* job with a little bit more meat to it. If they had something else that I could apply for, I would be more than willing to do any necessary training required. They did! A lead product specialist/trainer position was available and, to my amazement, they offered me the job. For eight years I traveled the country, stayed at fabulous hotels, trained on the BMW and MINI line and was able to coach and train their sales staff. What an incredible ride for a girl who grew up in the small town of Davie, Florida!

After eight years of being on the road came marriage and the associated settling down. Although there were mixed feelings, it was definitely time for the extensive traveling to come to an end. Not sure where to go from here, I asked my mom to keep an ear open for any full-time opportunities. Unbeknownst to me, she had passed my resume on to a contact at a well-known bank. They were hiring a financial specialist. Mind you, I had never had any banking or financial experience, but I did have leadership and sales experience. Nervously sitting in the waiting room with all of these men and women with four-year degrees and expensive suits, I just told myself that if this job were meant for me I would be offered it. If not, there would be something else in store. Well, after three months and numerous interviews, I was offered the job. With this position I was able to obtain two security investment licenses plus insurance and annuity licenses, and learn all about the retail and investment world.

The banking world is different from when I started four years ago. In the beginning I felt as if I were able to really help my clients with long and short term plans, and assist them in achieving their objectives. I was able to tailor plans that suited them, and to recommend things that would fit within their goals. But with all of the banking industry bailouts and changes in guidelines, the climate became one of wanting to see the numbers without care or concern about how they were obtained. Programs were to be pushed whether clients needed them or not. I am not a big fan of that method and I like to sleep at night, so I have continued to serve my customers the way I would want to be treated. Meanwhile, there is a ton of pressure coming from the top.

And that is what gave me the push to become an inventor. My light bulb flash came when I realized that if I could get something else going, I could leave my position with the bank and do my work from home. My goal was an ideal position for myself that incorporated balance among the important components of my life, and at the same time earned significant income.

Developing a new design for a teething pacifier, I began a patent search to make sure the device had not been replicated. Having no idea what I was doing, numerous phone calls were made with the U.S. Patent Attorney's Office to walk me through the necessary steps.

As I worked my way through this maze, an unexpected event occurred when a gentleman came into my office at the bank and asked if he could talk to me about my patent. I had never seen him before, but a work associate had told him a little about what I was doing and he was interested in offering guidance and assistance. I soon learned this man was a successful inventor with over thirty years of experience in doing his own patents. He was and continues to be a huge help with his wealth of knowledge, and has served as a mentor throughout the entire process.

I have always wanted to work for myself and visualize this possible patent as a way of doing just that. Family is super important to me and being there for my children and their activities is one of my top priorities. I believe getting this product on the market would give me the financial freedom and time I am looking for.

Despite the pitfalls, after four years I still consider banking a great position, with a few fellow employees who are like family. Meanwhile, we have expanded our family at home. Our son just turned two and our baby girl arrived in late March 2010. They have truly been a blessing in many ways, but their births have also opened up another business opportunity. Since we have had our son, I have been on the hunt for a teething device that works on all the teeth, not just the molars as in my first design. I have yet to find one, so I drew one up myself. While I am on maternity leave for my daughter I am working on a prototype for this enhanced item, and have contacted vendors interested in selling our product.

If you continue to wonder, life will always open new possibilities, incorporating what is most important to you. An idea becomes a design. A prototype becomes a product. A new invention may be marketed. One inspiration leads to another. I can now take my ideas from conception to creation. Who knows…this could be the beginning of a whole new career!

Dialogue in Black and White

Diane Halpin

Diane Marie Halpin is a licensed physical therapist, a cancer survivor, a wife and mother of four children, active in church, family, school, and various sport and outdoor activities. She grew up in Detroit but has lived in many other places, including Atlanta, Georgia; Chaska, Minnesota; and Mason, Ohio: transfers demanded by her husband's career. Each move meant, once again, making a home in a new place. She also happens to be one of my sisters, so it was with great interest that I read her perspective on her chosen topic of growing up in Detroit. Diane is a survivor in more ways than one.

I was born on November 1, 1960, in the city of Detroit. My mom says she took her six young children trick-or-treating and then came home and went into labor with me. I was to be the seventh of twelve children raised in a three-bedroom, brick bungalow with a fenced in yard and an occasional dog. My parents never had much money but I never really worried about it. There was always plenty to eat and hand-me-downs to share. Our family did not have a lot of rules or curfews, but we learned by example and a sense of being in this thing together.

In the 1960s our country—and the city of Detroit in particular—was going through a time of great unrest. President John F. Kennedy had been assassinated in 1963, followed by the murder of his brother Robert in June 1968. Dr. Martin Luther King Jr. spoke on TV and we heard him on the radio. The Civil Rights movement was in full force. At the time, I had no idea what all the talk was about or how it would impact my life on a historical level but also on a personal one.

I believe we make choices daily, both conscious and unconscious, that shape our lives and who we become as human beings. We choose our friends, our spouses, our careers, our faith, and our political persuasion. Eventually we become adults who reflect the choices we have made. I think some of our choices are very deliberate and well thought out, and others just happen out of life's circumstances over time.

I remember when my husband got his first job. It was all very exciting not to be in college anymore and to actually be receiving a paycheck. One of the questions his employer asked was "Would you be willing to relocate?" He checked the "Yes" box and thought nothing more of it. This choice, which was given very little if any consideration, and done in order to look like the ever-willing employee, became something that changed the life we would have with our family. Seven moves and twenty-two years later, I wonder about the life we would have had if he had checked "No."

When my parents were raising their children in the 1960s in the city, they too made a choice, whether conscious or unconscious, that changed the person I would grow up to be. In 1967 there were riots in Detroit and people were scared. On the evening news, people were angry and hateful, and there was a lot of talk about the racial divide in the city and our country. The riots started when police raided an after-hours drinking club expecting to find four or five patrons, but instead walked into a party being given in honor of two Vietnam veterans. There were eighty-two people attending the festivities and the police proceeded to arrest them all. People were outraged at being kicked out of a place they felt was one of the few places they had to go. A few angry people started fires, vandalized and looted businesses, and stirred up the outrage that had been brewing for some time.

Historians look back on the riots and recognize four major causes of the unrest in the city: police brutality and harassment of the black community, lack of affordable housing, urban renewal, and economic inequality. The riots spread over a five-day period through Northwest Detroit and to the Eastside. In the end, the National Guard and the 82nd Airborne had to be called to end the violence. The riots left 43 people dead, 1,189 people injured and over 7,000 arrested. The effects on the people of Detroit would be felt for many years. The fact that this happened in our own backyard was frightening, and in some ways broadened the racial divide.

The city, post riots, experienced a phenomenon known as "white flight," meaning white families left the city in massive numbers; and by the early 1970s our neighborhood, like many others, was predominantly African-American. It seemed as if daily we would hear of friends moving, families moving, and we sadly said goodbye to the neighborhood as we had known it. We had to drive to the suburbs to visit our cousins and we lost touch with friends who left. My parents, however, decided not to follow the crowd to the burbs, but instead to stay in the city and raise their kids as best they could. I am not sure if they ever sat down and discussed whether or not this was the best decision for their children or if they had to stay for financial reasons. I remember as a child being angry with them that we could not move like some of our friends. I tried to make the best of it, but when my best friend Annie moved as well, I was crushed. Why couldn't we go to one of those big houses "in the country" with five or six bedrooms and more than one bathroom?

I first became aware that there were black people and white people when I went to kindergarten in 1965. I remember bursting in the front door of our house full of excitement after my first day of school to find my mom visiting with her sister. I was going on about the teacher, the activities, and all of the kids I had met when my aunt asked, "How many black children are in your class?" I had no idea and told her so; it had never crossed my mind. The next day I remember noticing for the first time and counting. I was now aware that many saw the world in terms of black and white and not just as people trying to make their way in the world.

When I was in the third grade there was a girl named Sharon who tormented me. She would pull my hair and call me names like *honky* or *white girl*. One day when I was walking home from school, she came up behind me and pushed me down and dumped my book bag. I remember feeling her kick me as I lay on the sidewalk watching all of my papers blowing down the street. I got up, collected as much of my stuff as I could, and ran home with my two skinned knees bleeding down my legs. My mom immediately came to my aid and cleaned me up and explained as best she could why some people lash out at people who are different from them. Perhaps, mom told me, Sharon had heard of mean things that white people had done and just saw all white people as the enemy. She also explained that this was known as "prejudice" and it was wrong.

Later in my education, my parents transferred all of us to our parish Catholic school. Though more disciplined, they could not escape the racial tension that existed at that time in our city. For the most part, our school was calm and felt very safe to me. There was a public school close by that would sometimes have early dismissal, and students would come by our school to harass us when we were out for recess. They were tough black kids who would come looking for the white kids. On one of those occasions they targeted my sister, whom they knocked down, kicked, and crushed her glasses. I recall everyone running to our school building, and parents and teachers trying desperately to get us all in to safety. I can see my sister sitting there, bruised and crying, with her broken glasses in her hand; and I was mad. I was angry that these kids hated us for no reason other than the fact that we had white skin. I hated *prejudice* and wanted to scream that we were nice people who did not hate them for being black. I was angry that day, but I was also comforted by the fact that our black friends in our school stuck up for us and tried to get us in the building. They defended me, they had my back, and I never forgot that feeling.

In the seventh grade, a new girl moved into our neighborhood and I was so happy to have a friend again. Her name was Fabienne and she was a beautiful African-American girl. She was one grade behind me, but after school we were inseparable. We spent the night at each other's houses, we did each other's hair, shared clothes and we talked about everything. Faby (as her friends called her) had a black father and a white mother of French descent. We had wonderful times going out shopping or to other public places and seeing people look at us and try to figure out which kid belonged to which adult. Fabienne's brother was with us at times and he was a light-skinned black child so this created even more stares! We would talk about people's reactions when we returned home and it was a great open dialogue in which we could all see the prevalence and also the ridiculousness and ignorance of racism.

During my junior high and high school years I had many experiences with friends, neighbors, and schoolmates of different races. I knew what it was like to be one of a minority in a group of people. I knew the feeling of being stared at and called names, but even with those negative experiences I felt blessed to have lived the childhood that I did. I always had a lot of friends, as did my siblings. Our house was full of people both black and white, and we learned how to pick friends based on the "content of their character." We had to deal with sibling fights, getting all of us through school, automotive strikes, and crime in the neighborhood; but we also celebrated together whenever one of us reached a special milestone like confirmation, graduation, or a special birthday.

The choice made by my parents so many years before changed the person that I would become. I do not feel that certain things can be learned from books, or from lessons taught by the best of teachers. I believe some lessons have to be lived to truly bring about change and character development. I thank my parents for toughing it out when so many left. My mom is now a widow, and still lives in our three-bedroom bungalow in the city. She knows all of her neighbors—black, white, Jamaican, or other—and has many friends from Bible Study and church. Most of her children live in the cities that have grown up surrounding Detroit. We occasionally discuss the idea of finding Mom an apartment in the suburbs, but she always chooses to stay. And why not, it is her home.

Two Defining Hours
Reverend Elizabeth Hart Frazier

The first time I heard Rev. Frazier speak was at an American Association of University Women (AAUW) luncheon where she provided a lovely invocation before the meal. She had a beautiful way of including all faiths and incorporating the natural world into her grace. A couple of years later, I found myself seated next to her at a scholarship fundraiser with the same organization. She introduced herself simply as "Elizabeth." I found her to be an intelligent woman, passionate about religion and politics and committed to her responsibility as a cleric to represent women's issues. Elizabeth would like young women to recognize the struggles of their predecessors for rights they may take for granted, and after nearly a century of living, she is here to tell the tale.

Unordained, I walked into the room, facing the Jesuit priest, the rabbi, and twenty assorted Protestant clergy from a variety of denominations, entirely male, busily discussing matters related to the female body.

My 1969 appointment to the Religious Advisory Committee of Planned Parenthood - World Population came immediately as the executive of Church Women United reacted to my statement, "I am a displaced parsonage wife with a Yale University Divinity School degree and would like a place to count."

The executive grinned as she announced, "I have just the place for you," and then gave me her own position representing a loose organization of millions of Christian women on the Religious Advisory Committee of PP-WP.

Two hours later the meeting ended with my having said barely a word, aware that several of the clergy had degrees from narrowly-focused denominational theological schools, while I sat there with a degree from what was in the nineteen forties the premier theological school in the country, known worldwide for its scholarly, ecumenical faculty.

Realization hit. Ordination — which I had avoided for thirty years — was required to declare officially, "I bring denominational support, an excellent university degree, and most importantly the critical diversity of inhabiting a female body; this committee needs my input."

From the 1940 May day when I, six months pregnant, walked across the platform at Yale's Woolsey Hall to receive one of the first seven or eight theological degrees granted to women, I never really considered the goal of ordination.

In 1940 few denominations ordained women. In the early years I knew two women who served exceedingly small churches. One, with her husband, was the subject of a five-page article in *The Ladies Home Companion*, a major monthly of the day; the others were permitted to serve communion, especially at the women's district meetings. For that I could not see making a chasm between me and the women of the church my husband, Donald, served. A supportive husband, four healthy children, the church family and a busy telephone constantly creating new opportunities were enough. The world came to me.

Life is ever evolving. As I left the meeting I felt a compelling Call to speak responsively for the health and justice needs of those who inhabit a female body. How had I arrived so thoroughly at the conviction that I needed to challenge the thinking of representatives of much of Christendom?

Early interest was sparked as a teenager as I overheard whispering around Mother's bridge tables about a boy wandering among the clotheslines seeking women's underthings; those girls deprived both of schooling and reputation because of unwed pregnancy; and a husband's indiscretions affecting a wife's childbearing. In my parents' household, direct sexual questions received factual answers given in correct language. Knowledge was considered protection, not a guide to promiscuity.

Oberlin, the first college in the country to educate women equally with men, had a learning curve: they admitted black males two years before they admitted females. Robert Fletcher's seminar course on the New York state women's movement of the eighteen hundreds made a lifelong impression, for it underscored the years, labor, heartbreak and even violence involved in the effort to change long-established beliefs and actions. I quoted his writings frequently as I spoke on Planned Parenthood matters.

At Yale, Roland Bainton's church history was a constant reminder that all people, clergy included, are partial in their understanding and interpretation of the world we live in. Bitter wars have been fought to make particular perspectives prevail. Dominant patricidal language usage was a serious hazard in women's assessment of ourselves.

The sixties found our family once more in the Yale sphere as the Divinity School field work supervision provided by my husband as the minister of the West Haven Church was upgraded for a time to YDS faculty status. YDS interns needing on-hands training flocked across the river.

One child remained in the local school system; interns were everywhere so I was free to use time as I saw fit. Boards of Family Service, YWCA, AAUW, and shepherding the birth of West Haven's chapter of American Field Service compelled thinking and filled my time.

The quiet request of Ruth Bainton for me to serve on a small committee whose goal was finding a family to challenge Connecticut's repressive Comstock contraceptive laws became a dominant thrust of my life. Estelle Griswold, whose "right to privacy" approach made it to the Supreme Court of the United States, chaired that group. Roe vs. Wade, a 1965 Court ruling that the constitutional right to privacy extended to a woman's decision to have an abortion, still survives today midst violence, hope and fear. In 1965 the Yale-trained lawyer who prepared the brief was prohibited by gender from appearing before the U.S. Supreme Court. A male Yale professor was given that responsibility. A second committee member, determined that we widen our horizons while we waited for legal action, called weekly saying, "I want you at the School of Forestry at four p.m. Thursday. Paul Erlick is speaking on "The Population Bomb," or "Masters and Johnson on Sexual Health." The complexity of the right of privacy issue was present from the beginning.

Challenges hit indiscriminately, changing a family, community and individual potential. Donald's invitation to serve on the National Boards of our church meant an uprooting move to Old Greenwich, both an easy commute to the City and home of his parents for thirty-five years. Our welcome as lay folk into church and community was delightful. Within months I was placed on the Missions Committee with its thousands of dollars to allocate.

In 1971 a several-year project came to fruition. Several years before I had asked an assistant YDS dean, "What can I do to change thinking at this school with fifteen hundred dollars?" For a lifetime I have been grateful that instead of laughing, he suggested a ten-week seminar on subjects of interest to women and offered an auditorium and secretarial help.

A committee of three YDS women found speakers on overpopulation, Carolyn Byrd and finance, law, abortion, contraception, gender equality and religion. Carolyn Byrd's "Born Female" brought the entire Greenwich Missions committee to YDS for dinner and the Byrd speech. As the series ended, downtown Yale asked YDS, "What have you done in the public domain?" The women's ten-week seminar series attended by 2000 people was their only offering. Foundation grant appeals were written on that series for the next four years.

The degree was a plus. Service as an officer and member of both Fairfield and New Haven Associations of the

Congregational Christian churches made me known to those with the decision-making power of ordination, alerted me to appropriate language, and made road blocks to ordination without a local Call (to serve a congregation in need of a minister) visible. The head deacon of the largest, most generous church in the Connecticut Conference wanted to see me as the first woman to be ordained in the Old Greenwich Church. (At last count more than sixteen women have since been ordained in the Old Greenwich Church.)

Ordination to serve on a national committee instead of a local church was a stumbling block. However, everyone took a leap of faith and the unusual call was honored. The ecumenical congregation at my ordination service included Planned Parenthood executives, members from previous congregations, Dominican sisters, Yale faculty, clergy, and a most supportive family. The New Haven Register's Society Page carried a half-page article and picture—the gift of an AAUW journalist friend using the only place available in 1972 for women's news.

Any change generates unexpected consequences. Within weeks, all churches in the Connecticut Conference were requested to have an ordained woman in their pulpit at least once during the year. There I was with little competition and many one-day invitations. I became a bridge person for women wanting to enter the ministry from the pulpit level rather than through religious education. Unfortunately, many perceive the pulpit as of more worth than oversight of the church school.

Donald's and my lives have been enhanced by shared attention to these serious health and governmental issues. Oberlin, Yale and sixty-four years of marriage seemed but a beginning in the thought process. Standing on a Vero Beach balcony watching the space shuttle pierce the sky challenges medieval views of Heaven; plate tectonics explain our earthquakes but place us on an unstable planet. Psalms underscore the shortness of life on this earth.

At ninety-five I do not expect to see resolution of the complex issues surrounding Roe vs. Wade. Partial contributions from all sources are to be respected. Evolvement is powerful. Hope that I have been a contributory to the whole comforts me.

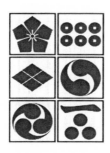

Déjà vu Iran

Ellen M. Rantz

Ellen was part of a creative writing group I joined when I first moved to Florida. I soon learned she was an interesting and multi-faceted person. From Plymouth (and possessing the look of a sturdy pioneer), she has returned to the Northeast many summers to do American Revolutionary War enactments. She is a talented artist specializing in pen and ink drawings, presenting her work in over fourteen national shows. Recently Ellen has picked up the art of fossil hunting in the area where she lives, once a Florida Cypress swamp, and way before that, a saltwater sea. But she chose to write about her time living in the foreign land of Iran.

About five years ago, before we moved permanently to Florida, my present husband, Carl, and I were invited to attend a local historical society dinner and lecture. The event was held at the Elks club in Fort Pierce, Florida. Seated around us at a long metal table were regular members of this group, to whom we were promptly introduced by my husband's niece. We exchanged the usual greetings and salutations and then proceeded to enjoy a tasty meal of baked chicken with all the trimmings.

When I finished my meal I left the table to go to the powder room. It was there that I spoke to a woman who had been sitting diagonally from me at the table. Her name was Marion. When I asked her if she were a native Floridian, she said that she was from half-way round the world. To my great surprise, Marion said that she was born in Mashad, Iran. I told her that my son, Reza, was born in that holy city as well, and that I had lived there close to thirty years ago with my first husband, Abdollah, an Iranian; daughter Mensorah age four, and son Reza age one, for four years. What an unbelievable experience to have met someone who once lived in the same obscure place in the world as I had!

Marion proceeded to tell me that she had lived at the Presbyterian Mission Compound for eighteen years until she left for college in Canada. She received her primary and secondary education from missionary teachers and learned to speak English and Farsi very well. Later in her life she was asked by the United States government to translate written documents, as there were not many people in the 1930s who could do this job. She had a very interesting life at the Compound and made many Iranian friends, as well as meeting missionaries and doctors from all over the world.

How surprised I was when Marion told me her father had been head surgeon at the Compound Hospital. They lived in the same house as my good friend, Mary Harvey, who was director of the Mission Hospital when I lived in Mashad. Although Marion had never met Mary Harvey personally, she had read in the Mission newsletter about her good works at the Mission Compound and at the Leper Colony Hospital on the outskirts of town. The sad news that Marion gave to me was that Mary had passed away about two years before.

We spoke briefly about our experiences at the Presbyterian Mission Compound and planned to meet again at her home to see the photographs she had taken during her life in Mashad.

Carl and I arrived at her home and were greeted in true Persian style, with iced tea, fruit and sweets while she told us the story of her life. Marion was born at the Mission Hospital, which at that time—in 1916—had four doctors in residence. She showed us three albums of photographs, some dating way back to the late eighteen hundreds when the Mission first opened. I had known this place so well as I, too, had been a temporary resident at Mary Harvey's Compound home while convalescing with hepatitis A. Mary was my nurse, and she hired a young Iranian doctor who was educated in Canada to come and administer liver shots. She made every attempt to make my life as comfortable as possible.

There were three residences on this block-long compound. However, from 1969 to 1973, the time I was living in Mashad, only one residence had occupants. Mary lived on the second floor of a two-story, mud brick house that was covered in an ivy-type plant and looked like a huge English cottage. Cathy and Dale and their two small children lived on the first floor. Seeing these photographs brought to mind the whole Presbyterian Mission Compound experience.

The Compound was only four blocks from where I lived. When my husband went to work and my household chores were done, I bundled up my children and visited friends practically every day. I would first come up to the ten-foot-high metal gate. One had to press the buzzer and then wait for someone to answer so that you could be identified and allowed entrance. Inside the gate there was a one-story building where Dale had his office. He kept the books for the Mission and worked on finances, paying bills and issuing checks.

Mary asked me to teach an art class for four young Iranian women whom she was instructing to be nurses aides. I was to help them make posters about health so they could bring them to the villages where they would be working. The young women were very good students, and expressed an interest in making a stuffed teddy bear. I made them a pattern and we had a great time with this project. Naturally I had to teach this class in Farsi, which I learned to speak quite well by my third year in Iran. I also received a paycheck from the Presbyterian Mission in New York for my "labor," which was really a joy to do.

One of the residences maintained as a guest house for visiting missionaries had a swimming pool. A couple of American friends, who were also married to Iranians, would bring their children over and lunch with my children and me around the pool. We would all agree how lucky we were to have a place like the Compound to escape to for a respite from living in a totally different kind of world.

All of these stories and more were shared during that first visit with Marion. We were able to speak about our experiences and what Mashad was like while she was living there; and by showing her the photographs I had taken over the years, how much it had changed. She had not been back to Iran for nearly forty years.

By the time I met Marion, Carl and I were only coming to Florida during school vacations. I was a public school art teacher at the time, and the duties and commitments of work still consumed me. I finally retired in 2003. We were able to see her only a few times after, as we were busy selling our home up North and moving to Vero Beach, Florida. Marion and I kept in touch by writing and calling one another once in a while.

I do remember visiting her at Heathecoat Botanical Gardens in Fort Pierce, Florida, where she volunteered working on the plants. She was eighty-six years old at the time. I still have a photograph of her happily amongst the flowers, dressed in her gardening smock, sunhat and gloves. Marion was given an award for her own yard, which was filled with native Florida plants. It was beautiful and lush, with birds and butterflies in abundance. About a year ago Marion sold her place and is now in an assisted living facility. It is not far from her former home with the award-winning garden, where cherished memories keep it close.

It's Greek to Me

Erasmia Vlastos Novotny

Erasmia, or, as all the kids in the neighborhood growing up in Detroit called her, Annette. Her sister Eleni was Helen. Her brother Michael was Mike. They were Greek and proud of it. Her grandmother spoke no English, but always nodded and smiled when Annette's friends stopped by. "Never on Sunday" was often playing on the stereo. Annette was tall and lanky as a girl, her thick black hair cut short, her youthful voice boisterous and edged with humor. A tomboy, she spent much more time playing baseball with my four brothers than dolls with me, but we all got together for hide-and-seek and other games. She could mimic the Beatles like nobody's business and sang a great rendition of "All My Loving" or "Twist and Shout." Annette grew up to become Erasmia Vlastos Novotny, a beautiful Greek-American who wants her culture to be remembered and its influence to be sustained. Fluent in the language, she has traveled to her native country — including the Isle of Crete where her family is from — so she knows the awesome beauty and the harsh realities of what she is trying to preserve a continent away. But she still has that great sense of humor.

Only one thing has been a certainty that has grounded me over the years. And that is the strength that has come from my Cretan heritage.

My life has been a journey of extremes, uncertainties, and challenges, but always with confidence and passion and an inspiring lesson.

I am fifty-five, have been married for thirty-six years, raised three children, started three businesses, lived through extreme economic conditions, and have battled breast cancer twice.

Growing up in Detroit, I was the youngest of three born to immigrants from the island of Crete. My parents brought us up in a very traditional Greek home and laid the foundation of public service by being active in several Greek organizations. My father, Constantine Vlastos, owned a restaurant supply company called C. M. Vlastos and Company on Detroit's riverfront. He designed the first versions of the heart-shaped candy boxes sold even today for Valentine's Day, which he named "The *Panemorpho*" (most beautiful) box. He and his boxes became well known throughout America's confectionaries. My father was a generous person. Having been penniless in his life, he was grateful for his good fortune and was first to help people. My mother, Diana, was known as the ultimate hostess, as she often entertained guests. Our home was always open for Dad's customers and business associates, family, Greeks and especially Cretans from around the country. Diana had a reputation of being able to feed an army and put out an elaborate spread at a moment's notice. As you can imagine, we had a very interesting and colorful life filled with love, fellowship and true Cretan *filoxenia* (a warmth and welcome for which people from the island of Crete are traditionally known).

A month before my fifth birthday, my father suddenly died of a stroke. Unfortunately, I have no recollection of my life with my father. I have seen many photos and heard numerous stories about him; even now occasionally when I travel to other states for business an old-timer will approach me and say, "I KNEW YOUR FATHER," raising his eyebrows with pride as if my dad were President of the United States. I am told that heads turned when he entered a room, and when he spoke he commanded an audience. He had integrity and was generous and the VLASTOS name was known from coast to coast. I remember the parties, the people, the house, food, toys, family and friends. If I could only hear his voice or remember anything from my years with him.

After my father's death our lives changed. Our extravagant life style had ended as we knew it, although my mom's spirit of entertaining continued. Even though we didn't have our father, she filled in the void by filling our life and home with friends and love.

My father's best friend was a man we knew as Uncle George who owned Delis Candies, a diner, soda fountain and candy store in Hamtramck, MI. My mom got a job there and found herself working twelve hours a day six days a week. We didn't see too much of her, but Friday night poker games at the store were something all the kids looked forward to. All the employees and some invited friends gathered in the back room for poker games that lasted into the early morning hours. While they were playing, we were too! Every week we had an ice cream fantasy night. We took turns being in charge and making each other sumptuous ice cream desserts. Unlimited, all night. When the adults were finished, they would come and find us sprawled throughout the diner sleeping in booths, our bellies distended, and overdosed on homemade ice cream. Before we left, Uncle George would line us up in front of his candy counter with an empty bag and tell us to walk through and fill up with our favorite candies. He was at the end waiting to say goodbye to us, and if he saw our bag was not full, we had to go through the line again. Torture, you can only imagine. Another example of Cretan *filoxenia*.

A few years later our mom remarried and became Diana Verykokakis. She thought he loved her and he thought she had money. (Both far from the truth!)

Looking back, I can see how hard it was for my mom to raise us. Working so many hours while trying to keep up her home, keeping track of our lives, and taking care of a new husband who had no interest in any of us or our home—*and he didn't drive*.

In the mid-1960s my mom purchased a well-known Greektown restaurant in Downtown Detroit, the Laikon Café. There, as a young teen, I spent many hours after school and on weekends. I began to appreciate my "Greekness." I fell in love with the food (a big problem!), music, and the traditions and customs that make up our rich heritage.

After high school graduation in 1972, I took my first trip with my family to our homeland. My mother had not been back since 1938. She had not seen one of her brothers since then. They were so excited to see us that we got the royal treatment from everyone we met. I discovered villages with no plumbing, outhouses, no electricity, and no air conditioning. I had to brush my teeth in the morning with trickling water from a spigot outside, and I cringed at the thought of the long bus ride with standing room only in a country that didn't know underarm deodorant. During that same trip I discovered the bluest of blue skies, bottomless crystal clear saltwater beaches, the vibrant flavors of fresh fruits and vegetables grown in the rich Mediterranean soil, and lots of family I had never met before. I will never forget the delicious smell of *souvlakia* cooking at the local *taverna* and music that filled the village…and my soul.

A part of me knew I belonged there and that someday I would be back.

When I returned to the U.S., I drowned myself in Greek music and reading and writing Cretan Poetry called *Mandinathes*, simple four-line poems that tell a story. I began making plans to go back to Greece the following summer to attend college there for a year or two. That spring I met my future husband, my trip was canceled, and the rest is history. We married a year later. I was nineteen and he was twenty-four. Five years later we began our family.

Life has been a journey of circumstances and uncertainty. Never having real direction, I have held many jobs and experienced many opportunities. With a combination of luck, good timing and quick thinking, I became a small business owner in my late twenties. Mark Twain once said, "All you need in this life is ignorance and confidence." That's me!

My husband was laid off from Ford Motor Company just as my sister and I launched "The Gold Connection," selling wholesale gold to retail customers and at-home parties. As my company grew by leaps and bounds, my husband was going from job to job, most of which provided no medical coverage and few benefits. My sister, a telephone company manager, then saw she couldn't keep up with the hours needed to contribute the time and energy required for our gold business, so she turned it over to me and it evolved into Pearlcraft Manufacturing, a home-based company providing jewelry and department stores with pearl and bead merchandise and services. Business boomed during my thirties and forties and life was good.

My three children were doing well in school and my husband was back at Ford's (which was thriving during that time). A small inheritance in Greece led to us building a home there near relatives, which has provided numerous unforgettable vacations. Just when everything in life was finally in synch I received the bombshell. At age forty-five I was diagnosed with bi-lateral breast cancer. The most challenging—and at the same time most fulfilling—chapter of my life had begun.

Suddenly everything on my agenda came to a screeching halt and the obvious took precedence. Waking up in the recovery room following a double mastectomy with my family around me, I had the profound feeling of "it's now or never." Realizing how important time is, and that my clock may be moving faster than ever, I decided to keep on my "to do" list a passionate project I had become involved in: developing a directory of Greek businesses and professionals for our community. Whatever my fate was, I had to prove to myself and to others that we could bring ourselves together and put a plethora of information in one first-quality publication, not only to promote our successes, but to honor our heritage.

Creating a Greek community reference directory had been a goal of mine for years. It was spurred on after spending all day on the phone after moving to a new neighborhood, trying to find a Greek school nearby. Why should it be so hard? I was sure someone more qualified than I would have attempted and completed such a list by now. Not! Some cited the reputation Greek people have of not being supportive of their own, yet they all felt such a publication was needed and encouraged me to venture on. A light when on in my head. Why not me?

With the help and encouragement of my good friends, I learned the publishing business from the bottom up. I spent a great deal of time during my cancer recovery learning Adobe Photoshop, PageMaker, and gathering information for my new endeavor. I began sifting through yearbooks, church directories and phone books, looking for Greek-owned businesses. I spent countless hours making calls and sending faxes and letters, asking for support and information for the project. To see the schools, churches, restaurants, businesses and professional members of the Greek Community represented in one directory gave me a great feeling of pride and accomplishment. More importantly, it showed others the power and influence we can have if we work together.

In conjunction with the Metropolitan Greek Connection Business Directory and Reference Guide, MALISTA.COM was developed. The publishing business proved to be very expensive, time consuming and limited in readers; but websites are inexpensive, potentially lucrative, and available to the world 24/7. I acquired an equally enthusiastic partner, and yet another business was born!

After seven years I got the cancer diagnosis again. This time strong chemo treatments really knocked me off my feet. Out of six treatments, I ended up in the hospital four times, two of those with pneumonia and dangerously low white blood cell counts. The whole time was quite a blur and I really would like to try to forget it, but a few things come to mind that helped me through it all. LOTS of family around, my best buddies visiting and calling to keep my mind busy, and I NEVER stopped working any of my jobs—jewelry, secretary of The Pancretan Association of America, and website—even in the hospital; and lots of water to flush the chemo out of my system. And music! During this time, at the age of fifteen, my son played the piano and guitar for me, filling the house with melodies and soothing my soul.

Today I am still the National PAA Secretary and I will concentrate my efforts on the Malista.com website, which highlights Detroit's Greek identity, brings people together from around the world, and allows me to celebrate my heritage in a creative and modern way. My Greek heritage shapes me and gives my life profound meaning that goes to the very heart of who I am. It has sustained me through everything. Inside I am still a Detroit girl, an American woman, a wife, mother and friend. My husband is retired, the kids are grown, my mother is ninety-six, and I'm still alive!

It's good for all of us to remember not only what we can accomplish together, but what a difference we can make as individuals. You don't have to have money or expertise, just passion in what you want to do, faith in yourself, and determination to reach your goal. For me, the secret ingredient in this formula has always been the love and support of family and friends. Listen to your heart and take action on what means the most to you. Pay attention to that light in your head signifying inspiration. And ask yourself, "Why not me?"

Diamond Mosaic

Gail Lois Jaffe Satuloff

I first met Gail Lois Jaffe Satuloff at a welcome tea for new members of the American Association of University Women (AAUW) around 2002. Neither one of us was a "joiner"; subsequently neither one of us really fit in or found a place among this group of proper, political, mostly older women. But we found each other, and a friendship bloomed that has continued to flower over the years. Gail gives me Miami perspective (where she grew up), Jewish wisdom (part of her culture), artistic and new age philosophy (influenced by the Virgin Mary and Carl Jung), and bawdy humor (we laugh out loud). She might show up in her convertible, wavy blonde hair flying, dressed in high-heeled sandals and glitz; but she provides ageless truth and sustenance. What's not to love?

Emerging from the center of the Earth, pushed by volcanic emissions and extreme pressure on the carbon of which it consists, the Diamond can be found within the molten lava. This is after being subjected to extreme heat and pressure as well as a series of processes and transformations taking millions of years.

Then there's the mining and the cutting, polishing, design, setting, and commerce involved in the finished product. The details of this complicated and miraculous process can be supplied in detail by scientists and gemologists—I am only interested in the metaphor at present: that each of us embodies this miraculous journey of the Diamond.

We, as women, have all been subjected to intense pressure and have surfaced against all odds into the individual Diamonds we are. Some of us are cut and polished more precisely and artistically and perhaps are shown in better settings, but each a diamond nonetheless.

I believe the metaphoric journey of the diamond is repeated numerous times over one's lifetime as more original material from our psyches is brought to our consciousness to transform us at the right time. At the time of this invitation to write about myself, I am in a period of reflection, as more carbon is being brought up to be transformed. The benefit of my five-and-a-half decades has slowly given me the wisdom to hold the hope and vision of the bigger picture as the process emerges. Carbon can be awfully dense—ah, the clarity and light of the diamond!

Well, before I wear out the metaphor—if I haven't already— let's move on to my personal journey and perspective, which is, after all, the only thing we can share with others. I was born with artistic gifts and an exquisitely sensitive relationship to my environment that enabled me to perceive and take into myself many things that have caused me much suffering and sadness. I carried much of this for a long time. Through determination, hard work, belief in my value, and the ability to transform and grow; receiving much guidance, support, and experience, I became a psychotherapist.

Over the course of thirty years, I have worked with people suffering from addictions, and clients with post-traumatic stress disorder (debriefing bank employees who had been through bank robberies and other victims of workplace violence). I have done drug evaluations in prisons, wellness seminars for corporations, supervisor trainings and consultations, and private practice with individuals and couples. Summarizing thirty years of experience in a paragraph makes for rather dry reading, but the magic and poignancy of having the privilege of interacting with so many people on such a deep level was rewarding and profound.

On a personal level I have experienced excitement, transformation, turmoil, questioning, travel, friendships lasting decades, love, painting, creativity, and marriage; each adding more facets to the diamond of my life. I choose to see my life as a mosaic, so that I don't over-identify with any one aspect, and it makes me feel more free.

A decade ago I wrote and illustrated a book with the love, support, and encouragement of my husband, Barth. *The Enchanted Mirror*, which combined aspects of my two loves, art and therapy, is a book about seeing one's Self in a Cosmic Mirror — a reflection in which one fully participates in creating — trying to reduce the need for external validation. Alas, another irony. I REALLY wanted people to like my book — so much for eliminating the need for external validation! Many people do like it, and that's also appreciated.

Barth and I relocated from Miami to Vero Beach eight years ago to soak in the natural beauty and quiet of this town, with my intention being to paint and write. That was not entirely in the cards; quiet and peace often evade all of us. My husband and I started our wedded life by getting married on the eve of Hurricane Andrew in Miami, but that's the subject of another essay!

I took a position at Hospice as a bereavement counselor. I guess I still wasn't ready to give up my profession. I met so many dedicated and sensitive people, both colleagues, patients and families; and learned so much about death and grief, family, spirituality, surrender, and so many other things I can't begin to describe. That experience affected me in ways I couldn't imagine, and helped to bring about my own encounter with unprocessed and unresolved grief, which I believe most of us carry with us, buried deeply. I realized my work in that field was completed and it was time to move on to other explorations.

The past six years have been an interesting journey. My husband and I built a home in Colorado. I have painted and exhibited my work. I have studied and practiced yoga and obtained a certification which has deepened my practice. I take belly dancing classes, work out, and devote myself to my marriage, our three dogs (dogs are God's gift), friendships, and my spiritual practice of trying to integrate mind-spirit-body — quite a slippery task!

I find myself in an interesting part of my life as old ways of defining myself slip away and I attempt to integrate the experiences of my life, to enjoy the interplay between ego and soul, public and private, will and surrender, immersing myself in Time rather than racing against it. It is a time of inner focus within, where deep shifts are taking place.   A melding of spiritual, material, pain, joy, uncertainty and disappointment are all being pressured and heated by the forces of Truth, Faith, and Love.

I believe each of us must remain true to our own unique process of becoming the Diamond that we are intended to be, without giving up on ourselves during the uncertain times. Concepts such as *mid-life, old,* or *young* should not restrict us from polishing our Diamond and insuring the most attractive setting possible, so it will be its most beautiful when presented to God. I believe each one of us sits on a shelf in the Cosmic Jewelry Store, waiting in the dark for the One who will walk in and choose us.   In our dark moments, we believe we are too flawed to be chosen.   In the light that is inside us always, we know we are already chosen.

O Pioneer?

J.J. Wilson

J.J. Wilson was seated in a white wicker chair, her hands to her cheeks with a warm smile on her face, on the cover of the Vero Beach newspaper 32963 when I first saw her. The article was about her home on the barrier island, built as a winter cottage in the 1930s, complete with lemon trees and iron gate and character, in the area known as Riomar. I sent her a letter and asked if we could meet. We have since become friends. When I asked her to write about being a pioneer, I had no idea I would receive a missive on her years in California, where she still spends summers. J.J. is a "free thinker" and I neglected to define "pioneer."

Cynthia described me as a "pioneer," but I am much more of a follower. It was at a predictable time and place in the history of women studies that I got "converted," namely in the early 1970s at one of those convention hotels in Chicago where a panel featuring such women writers as Tillie Olsen, Adrienne Rich, Alice Walker spoke to members of the Modern Language Association, a professional organization for college teachers and graduate students of literature. What did they say on the fateful night? You can find it all on the web by googling Adrienne Rich, "When we dead awaken," but what is important to this story is that their fiery words set flame to our dry tinder and we all dispersed back to our various schools burning to change the male-dominated curriculum and damn the torpedoes...

Indeed some of the younger and more vulnerable professors did suffer consequences—not getting awarded tenure, for example—for both what they did and how they did it.

However, my college, Sonoma State, founded in 1965 in Northern California, was like a new pioneer village (there's that word again) where faculty, staff, and students were encouraged to experiment, innovate, venture out. I received nothing but positive feedback for my first tentative and not very daring courses in "Women in Literature" (where the syllabus featured *Antigone* and *Emma Bovary* as well as Jane Austen and George Eliot). It took me several radicalizing teaching semesters to realize there were enough good women writers to fill the entire syllabus and then some! When I see the fat anthologies now available to provide students with glimpses of the many, many women writers in English and also in World Literature, I thrill with pride; but in the early days, preparation for these never-before-taught-courses required making mimeograph copies of such hard to find texts as Zora Neale Hurston's *Their Eyes Were Watching God* or even Virginia Woolf's now iconic *A Room of One's Own*. If having hands purple to the wrist with mimeo ink is the mark of a pioneer, then maybe we were pioneering.

We certainly had no GPS on our journey, and no e-mail or Google either, but somehow we all kept in touch with our friends from that MLA meeting and gave one another support and information. How did we do it? A reformist adrenaline surged through our veins along with the mimeo ink; and we lugged briefcases full of materials to share at every meeting, formal and informal.

I remember my shock several years later while interviewing candidates for faculty positions in women studies to find that the young people specializing in this new field were chary of sharing their syllabi, insisting on holding a kind of intellectual patent on the material which in the early days we had all shared so gladly — as if at a recipe swap or a quilting bee.

One area in which my colleague Karen Petersen and I were indeed pioneers (if that means setting out into uncharted territory without proper tools or qualifications) was collecting slides by women artists. Though both trained in literature, we loved the visual arts; and fortunately Karen knew German and I knew French which helped us in our research and travel. My past experience in the '50s as a secretary at the National Gallery of Art came in handy too. My boss there, Erwin O. Christensen, wrote an ambitious book while I worked for and with him, "A History of Western Art." I typed that manuscript four times (and this was before word processors!), editing it down and writing picture captions — all tasks somewhat beyond my pay scale but wonderfully useful experience later when Karen and I were asked by Harper and Row to write a book on the history of women artists for them.

Of course, starting out on this project, we had NO idea that we were moving toward a New York publication, *Mlle* award, *Ms* mention, and travels all over (and Karen did not know she was going to be producing a baby in the middle of the manuscript preparation either! There we *were* pioneers, negotiating the inclusion for the first time of childcare costs into the publishers' advance.). In the beginning we were just drawn by the excitement of the hunt and by the biographies of these neglected geniuses, carrying our precious slides (beautifully reproduced for us by our school) around in a cigar box to show to the newly burgeoning women's studies classes in our area. The appreciative audiences could see with their own eyes visual evidence that women WERE doing art everywhere, at every time, and in all media. Their art and their lives were inspiring and instructive, sad and comic, and often seemed to illustrate a subtly different narrative of society than the given, i.e. male version.

This compelling slide show got us invited all over, even to North Dakota once in minus 8 degree winter. Karen's movements were somewhat curtailed by motherhood, but I gave the ever evolving lecture in England (where our book was published by the Women's Press) and even as far away as Dubrovnik at a women's conference there. One of the healthiest aspects of women studies was its openness to interdisciplinary projects and to people who like us were working out of our field of expertise. Truth to tell, no one was an expert in researching women in those early days and we all had that "Beginner's Mind" the Zen teachers admire.

Oh, it was hard work but at least we knew our efforts were needed to set the record straight, a tremendous incentive—as were the gleams in the eyes of artists in our audiences. All was not easy as puddin' and pie, of course. For example, we were held up at the Canadian border by customs because they feared our slides of "women artists" might well be pornographic (and some of them were pretty erotic!). We were isolated from one another and interrogated for several hours as to our purposes in going to Canada (though no waterboarding!) before a call to our host university set us free.

Then back on my own campus in an Our Bodies/Our Selves class, students were investigating their own vulvas using mirrors and speculums when the (woman) vice president appeared and stopped it, suggesting mildly that such explorations might better be done OFF campus if we wanted to be taken seriously as an academic subject... We did have to stage a student occupation of our Women's Studies trailer office to save that precious legitimizing space, as well as move heaven and earth to get a child care trailer added next door. On the other hand, the school librarians were able allies, ordering every new book, video, and magazine on the subject of women that were flooding out in the new publishing wave. They combined with other teaching faculty to organize a seminal lecture series called "Changing Woman," which was publicized in a stylish poster done for us by a budding feminist who worked in the Reprographics Dept. and moonlighted it for us. Needless to say, we were not a line item on any budget for some time and her work helped make us visible. When I tried to pay her an honorarium, she informed me that blue collar workers should also be permitted to volunteer for the cause — a good point and one of my many lessons during this university-wide and indeed community-wide collaboration.

What else did I personally learn from these exertions? To trust my instincts; to be willing to be criticized and even, ulp!, disliked; to be moderate; to not give up; and to recognize that others could be counted on to work for the common good (oddly enough, that was a biggie, perhaps because I was the oldest sibling and had usually gotten points by getting up early and doing all the heavy lifting...).

And now, in 2010 when there are sightings of new stars such as the brilliant 6'8" basketball player, Brittney Griner; or the versatile musician Esperanza Spalding, product of home schooling and a single mother; or that riveting performance artist Marina Abramovic, all of them geniuses with impunity; well I do wonder if they are not avatars of a new breed of women, helped into being by that process begun back in the Chicago hotel MLA meeting in 1971. How fortunate I was to be part of it! And thanks to you, Cynthia, for gently nudging us into writing about these heart-driven actions which we took with no guarantees of positive outcomes.

The Earth Mother

Josephine Hurst

Josephine Hurst is that rare combination of the scientific and artistic. Some of her many accomplishments and adventures are described here. There is no one subject to cover Josephine. She is an abstract of disjointed colors and pieces that somehow come together as a cohesive picture. Illness prevented her from writing about herself so I asked, and was granted, permission to write her piece.

When I first met Josephine I was a girl of fourteen. She was a striking woman, seated in the living room of her brother's home in Michigan, having just arrived from Florida for a visit. Her straight brown hair, barely held in a large clip, streamed down her back. She had a British accent. She drove a little red sports car. She spoke to me as if I were an adult. I was quite taken with her.

Years later, some time after I married her brother, we met again in Florida. Josephine was an accomplished artist by then.

Particularly interested in lines of motion, she found the perfect subjects in horses and greyhounds. She captured them in various poses: bolting, rearing, running free, caught in a moment of grace in plaster or bronze. Abstract forms of a torso or a wave were rendered in marbled pink, polished black and pearly white alabaster. Whimsy was not beneath her, as she produced colorful fish dishes and flowing galaxies on twelve-inch plaster plates.

When Jo came over for dinner she was just family, sipping a beer, appreciating the food, enjoying Richard's piano playing afterwards. She was comfortable at our home, located on one of the canals in the Citrus Isles of Fort Lauderdale, and in those days I saw her relax in our company. We loved to sit on the lanai late into the evening with candles for light, insects for sound, night-blooming jasmine for scent, dessert or an after dinner drink lingering on our taste buds.

Josephine fit into the old Florida scene easily, a warm presence blending with palm trees and salt air and seawater. A no-frills bohemian, artsy but unpretentious, she also fit the bill of the seasoned sailor, the free spirit; earth mother to all the artists, drifters, mavericks and misfits who found their way to her door. Dinner at her place was always casual and delicious. She didn't like to turn on the air conditioning, so we always dressed for a tropical night at Jo's. An accomplished cook, she knew the secret of fresh ingredients prepared simply. I remember wonderful tomatoes from containers on the patio, meatballs with lemon and veal, yummy fish suppers, desserts with mango and lime. An orchid from the yard decorated each place setting.

Her mother, Josephine Rita Carlin Hurst, lived a very socially conscious life but she was not a cook. If she was entertaining, her secret to a good dinner was to serve several cocktails prior. A librarian, a philanthropist, supporter of the arts, benefactor to young nuns, and wry literary enthusiast, she flew to Paris for a fun little getaway in the days when few used "airliners" and partied with the likes of Dorothy Parker. She once heard sirens signaling a fire in the neighborhood, donned her fur coat, and took a suitcase full of cash to the couple as they watched the flames consume their home. With a few words of comfort, she left the scene before they knew her name. In a five-thousand dollar investment bet with her husband, in order to "teach her about money" by seeing who would profit the most, Josephine Rita invested in the start-up company of a man she had heard about. His name was Ray Kroc. He was forming a concept that would become McDonalds, and Josephine Rita liked the idea. She thought "everyone should have a hamburger." She won the contest hands down.

So you see the stock from which Josephine is made. She and her three younger siblings learned to be independent at an early age. They were encouraged to try anything and were supported in their endeavors, particularly if they were academic, athletic, Catholic, or business related. Josephine became an accomplished equestrian. She obtained her Ph.D. in Physiology/Hematology at St. John's University in New York. She taught at the graduate and post-graduate level. She was Director of Research and Education at the Goodwin Institute for Cancer Research, Visiting Professor at the University of Bristol School of Medicine UK, and a visiting researcher at the Patterson Laboratories-Holt Radiation

Lab in Manchester, England. Studies of marine-derived cancer drugs followed, and work with the New York Ocean Science Laboratory. For years she led the life of an academic and a research scientist, receiving numerous grants and writing over twenty research papers.

All of this time, Josephine followed a dual career in art. But her work as a professional sculptor was like a spark inside that soon consumed everything. Raw materials, creating something from nothing, chiseling away the layers to reveal the form beneath — all of this fascinated her. She exhibited her work at several galleries, managed exhibitions of equestrian art at the Royal Palm Polo Club in Boca Raton, and formed a corporation called Equestrianarts, Inc. in 1981 to manage and sell her art. A number of awards for her sculpting and commissioned works followed. When most people would be considering retirement, she became fluent with computer graphics software in order to experiment with new digital art forms.

When I caught up with her again in Florida, her long hair was cropped but her worldly demeanor remained the same. She had been married, divorced, lived on a sailboat for twelve years exploring the Islands, and was a full-fledged professional sculptor. She had piloted her own plane, swam with dolphins, and slept under the stars if she chose.

Few have the wherewithal to live the life of a true artist. It is not conventional. Josephine's life has been full of accomplishment, sans children and traditional family. Recognition and fame have been hers with limited monetary reward, but it has always been enough to suit her. The reward is in the creation. She has lived with little and found contentment there. She is supportive of the aspirations of others and happy to mentor young authors and artists. She is liberal and open and gives you her whole attention. People flock to her.

It is early 2010 and Josephine is seventy-one. Emphysema is taking its toll for a lifetime of smoking; her health is failing her. She still checks the computer to keep in touch with extended family and friends. Breathing is difficult and she often needs the supply of oxygen strapped to her body. She was given a few months to live two or three years ago. Hospice welcomed her with open arms but eventually sent her home. Living in a small place on the canal close to where her brother once lived, she still greets a neighbor who lives on his sailboat in her "backyard," or accepts a kiss on the cheek from an old friend bringing homemade chicken soup. Art—Josephine's and others'—fills her otherwise modest home. Herbs and tropical flowers, once flourishing, languish a bit on the patio.

Something unfinished or perhaps some new awareness, a small comfort, a moment of enlightenment, an unexpected joy still awaits Jo Hurst.

Author's note: Josephine Marie Hurst died just before sunset on March 27, 2010. A family slide show that normally cycles five seconds per slide stuck on a photo of Jo sitting on the beach in Fort Lauderdale. In it, she is looking offshore at a sailboat and toward her beloved Bahamas. Perhaps, as a friend wrote, she came to say goodbye, things are good on the other side.

A Little Stardust in Our Lives

Joyce Levi

Joyce Levi is one of the thousands of people in the music, theatre and film industries who never make it to the big time, but reach for the stars just as hard as those who do. They make a living doing what they love best, and recognize that fame is an illusive combination of talent, luck and timing. But neither pop celebrities nor movie stars, Broadway nor Hollywood can corner the market on the one thing all actors and entertainment artists infuse into their lives: Stardust!

Whatever speaking or writing project I'm involved in, I use quotes. I own 35 wonderful books of quotations and nowadays frequently search the Internet for a new one. I love tagging along on some clever person's thoughts.

The title above is from words by former president Ronald Reagan, speaking of a time in his life when he portrayed other people on stage or in film. He said of audiences, "We've kept a little stardust in our mundane lives by identifying with make-believe characters in make-believe adventures in the house of illusion—the theatre." Actors and audiences are both stuffed with stardust.

Looking back from the age of 81 at a life filled with stardust is simply joyful.

In the 1930s, young lives were rich with moments of make-believe and "let's pretend." Saturday afternoon ten-cent picture shows (and a nickel for candy) brought drama and laughter to us, along with dreams of becoming movie stars.

Growing up in Birmingham, Alabama, there were not many opportunities to stretch personas with acting. Every little girl in our neighborhood took ballet and tap dancing lessons and performed in annual recitals. Real live audiences. And costumes. And applause. How heady!

In Miss Reagan's first-grade class I was in a short two-person play. And somewhere along the way I played a dandelion in a school pageant. When I was ten, I won a young poets award from the Alabama Writers Conclave and appeared onstage in front of 1,000 people to have my poem read aloud. As an eighth-grade senior I was again in a short play, and read a Bible passage at graduation. Not many chances to captivate an audience, but the lure was surely there.

During World War II, my family moved to Charlotte, North Carolina, for a brief time and Daddy's office was in the same building as a radio station. There was a contest to see which high school students showed possibilities of being radio talent. I won that one. Cold reading—"with expression," as my Aunt Lollie used to say—has always been easy for me, and I guess I bluffed my way through an excited, ad lib description of a downtown fire.

Moving back to Birmingham, I took high school drama classes, appeared in a few plays and was firmly caught. I wanted to be an actress. Preferably on Broadway, but Hollywood stardom would be acceptable as well. Stardust.

At Alabama College, now the University of Montevallo, I majored in *speech and dramatics,* as it was called back then, and was fortunate to be cast in challenging roles. I began working on eliminating my Southern accent. In those days Southern accents were okay for the character actress, the girlfriend down the street, not the leading lady.

During summer vacation following my freshman year, I received a letter and script from Trummy (department head Dr. Walter Trumbauer). The script was for *Electra*, the Greek tragedy by Sophocles, and I was to play the lead. Well! I was absolutely thrilled—until I read it. I couldn't make sense of the lines, the plot was boring and difficult to follow. Oh, no. I was devastated. This would ruin me.

With Trummy's gentle guidance, I learned how to perform in classic theatre, an area I quickly grew to appreciate and love dearly.

Actress Katherine Hepburn once wrote: "I think most of the people involved in any art always secretly wonder whether they are really there because they're good—or there because they're lucky." Luck has always been part of my theatre experiences. I'm considered a good actress as well, but how blessed to be in the right place with the right person. Toward the end of my junior year I attended a college arts series performance of *The Importance of Being Earnest*, produced by the respected Barter

Theatre of Virginia. Rebecca Jennings, a friend from Birmingham, had graduated from Alabama College and was working tech in professional theatre in Denver. Becky wanted to go backstage and meet some of the cast, so we did. The person she headed for was the lead actor/company manager, Owen Phillips. After congratulating him on the play's success, she badgered Owen that he ought to take me back to Virginia with the troupe, that I was a marvelous actress, on and on. Owen turned to me and said, "Write a letter to Barter, tell them you want to be an apprentice this summer. Be sure to mention my name because they get thousands of applications and automatically toss them without a personal reference." Luck. Stardust.

I wrote the letter, auditioned, and was accepted into the world of capital-T Theatre. The summer in Abingdon was filled with rehearsing, acting, working backstage, learning, and touring to small, nearby towns. At the end of the summer, Owen called me aside and asked me to stay with Barter, do the winter tour playing the lead in three different shows, and immediately become an Equity member.

"I can't," I said sadly, "I'm editor of the school paper this year. And I need to graduate." Owen thought I was crazy and maybe I was. Certainly naive. But my generation was the first in the family to attend college, and we all desperately wanted those diplomas.

So. Another year. A good one. More plays. More audiences. Diploma.

There was no money for New York, so I started working for the Birmingham Library and discovered the Shakespearean

Repertory Theatre. Ah, Juliet and Katherine and Lady Macbeth, and Bill Ozier, a brilliant director who honed the edges of my classical training.

One day the national tour of *Harvey* came to Birmingham and I had lunch with Barter friends Ernie Borgnine and Virginia Mattis, who were with the show. "What are you doing in Birmingham?" Ernie asked.

"Trying to raise money for New York," I replied.

"Forget that," he said, "call Barter and tell them you're on your way."

Laughing, I responded that I certainly could not do that. But I did, and played the national tour with Barter in the fall, mostly one-to three-night stands in small towns of many states. Adventures. Stardust.

I met my husband, Win Levi, when we played Washington, but that's another story.

In New York, I started doing musical theatre in a charming but clumsy off-Broadway take-off of *Oklahoma!*, called *Dakota*. Then another national tour, this time of major cities like Cleveland, Detroit, Montreal. And this time as an Equity actress. Stardust.

Win moved to New York and we started dating seriously, but since he told me on our first date that he wasn't the marrying kind, and I was not yet a Broadway star, I decided to head back to Birmingham. My first interview as a secretary was at a radio station and within a week I was on the air. For the next three years, I acted/played with Town and Gown community theatre. Then Win and I were married, and I was back in New York, where I worked briefly for a national radio syndicate, raised two delightful sons, and saw lots of good theatre. For several years before retirement I performed in and directed musical revues for a not-for-profit group.

Retiring to Vero Beach, Florida, in December 1983, in January Win and I both auditioned for the Vero Beach Theatre Guild production of *The Music Man*, and both were cast, beginning 26 years of delightful community theatre involvement. Treasure Coast talent is phenomenal, many former professionals end up here, and Riverside Children's Theatre is a superb training ground. Seven different publications have called the Guild "community theatre at its finest," and I firmly agree.

Here I've acted, directed, written news releases, published playbills and brochures, made speeches and posters, done radio shows and commercials, won acting and other awards, and been part of many enthusiastic audiences, cheering on neighbors and teachers and physicians and real estate agents and accountants, people from all walks of life, all collecting and sprinkling stardust as they make believe. Close to 300 people feel the pull and volunteer each year in some capacity at the Guild.

At the age of 81, I find few plays with roles for someone like me. The last leading role I had was in a Noel Coward show that was canceled when Hurricanes Frances and Jeanne raged around Vero over a three-week period. But I find tremendous satisfaction in performing occasional readings in church worship services, and doing radio interviews about theatre and what's happening both onstage and offstage.

Makeup is different nowadays. The smell of greasepaint, so familiar 50 years ago, is no longer around. But most other things have remained the same. Something about theatre satisfies the soul. Whether sitting in the audience or dressing room, waiting for places to be called, the lights to dim and curtain to rise, there is an excitement unmatched anywhere. For the actor: Will I do my best? Will they like me? For the audience: Will we laugh tonight? Will we learn? Will we cry? Will we grow? Will we go home singing?

What was it Reagan said? "We've kept a little stardust in our mundane lives by identifying with make-believe characters in make-believe adventures in the house of illusion—the theatre."

My whole life has been glowing with stardust. It still is. All kinds, all levels. Magic.

A blessing. A privilege. Simply joyful.

Pregnant Pause

Katie McGinnes

Katie McGinnes is the sister of Joe MacLellan, who married my sister Michelle. The MacLellan family has roots in Nova Scotia, and I have thoroughly enjoyed meeting parents Duncan and Mary, charming old aunts, and everyone in-between. Katie is feisty and funny and reminds me of a filly or young Scottish lass. But since I met her she has grown up, married Neil McGinnes (complete with clan wedding and men in traditional kilts), and together they welcomed their first child, daughter Mairi, on June 15, 2010. One thing that hasn't changed is her humor, and she is still that spirited lass. I guess that's two things...

Ponderings from the pregnant desk of Katie McGinnes

2.5 months along – Announcement to the cousins!

Neil and I will be adding a cousin to the clan in June 2010 (June 22 is the due date)! I am my mother's child and wrought with worry - and will take any prayers you send our way!!! The reaction I'm getting from many is positive, but it's those who know me best who react with laughter. Yes... I meant to do this!! hahaha...

So, to stay in line with my nature - I'll let you in on some of my experiences during the last couple months.

1. I am emotional and hungry – and shocked at the correlation between them!

    So food tastes different now - especially my favorite comfort (aka - hangover) food. I ordered my favorite one day, all excited to gorge myself on a chicken sub with fries and gravy, but alas... it tasted BAD, and I was so HUNGRY! I tried a few bites and gave up, crying. I was standing at the freezer crying and eating chocolate chip cookie dough ice cream (?!) when Neil walked in... confused. I, less than coherently, explained that I was very upset about this alien taking over my taste buds. Neil, not wanting anything to go to waste, responded by eating my sandwich and fries.

    My problem wasn't that he ate it, but how HAPPY he looked while eating it - I wasn't very nice... Thus began the new link between food and my ever changing emotional state.

2. Telling Mom and Dad was fun - and a bit scary. Telling Mom is easy, but Dad kinda stressed me a bit. I am forever his "little girl" and pregnancy is proof positive of... you know!!!

    Neil and I went for a visit to their house on Halloween. Dad was in his rocking chair, Neil and I on the couch, and Mom on a chair next to the couch with her crocheting. PaPa mentioned they're heading to JoJo's house for trick-or-treating with the wee ones (you can hear him in your head, can't you?) and I said, "Maybe next year you can come over to our house for trick-or-treating with your OTHER grandchild."

    Both of them were confused for a second with Mom saying, "Are you... Are you..." but the best reaction was Dad. He stopped rocking. Face went blank. I think he always envisioned yelling when I told him I was pregnant (i.e., "WHO DID THIS TO YOU" and comments of how he will hurt said destroyer of my innocence). He recovered quickly and asked when the baby was coming. Since then, it's been hard to contain them - I was sure it'd be in the Oran or Cape Breton Post before my 3rd month!

3. I am at High Risk because of... Advanced Maternal Age. I
    nearly kicked the doctor when he told me what AMA
    means.

    I am High Risk because I'll be 35 when I deliver. This
    means they want to scare the livin' daylights out of
    me with all these stats and tests and huge needles in
    my belly. Had I been born six months earlier it'd be
    smooth sailing.

4. I am scared I'm going to deliver a small elephant-sized
    baby who won't sleep because he or she is pumped full of
    sugar. Me... DIABETES? The digester of family-sized
    bags of Better Made BBQ chips? The avoider of all
    things sweet? Alas... yes.

    Typically, women aren't tested for gestational
    diabetes until their 3rd trimester, but a regular
    screening displayed indicators for me during the 1st
    trimester so they tested me. The thing is, one of the
    side effects of gestational diabetes diagnosed later in
    pregnancy is a larger baby. The baby sucks up all the
    sugar because there's little insulin to break it down,
    causing a hefty 10+ pound baby! Now, with my logic -
    if women who are typically tested, diagnosed and
    treated at 7 months pregnant have 10-pound babies,
    wouldn't that mean a woman diagnosed and treated at

2.5 months will have an even LARGER baby? This, and the need to purchase muumuus, freaks me out completely!!!

5. Food, Diabetes and Hormones - yes, food and hormones again. It's a big deal for me.

This simple sentence should explain all: *FRIES ARE BAD FOR ME.* Carbs are the diabetic devil. I'm told I don't need to cut them out completely, I just can't eat as many. ME... RESTRAINT??? It's just better not to let them near my plate... or Neil's. So try to imagine if Neil would like to order fries while out with me - see # 1 for a guess at my reaction.

6. I am the Designated Driver

This can come as a shock - but I've no problem *not* picking up the cocktails. I'm also fine with driving after all these years of NOT driving - I get it, it's about time! However, there is a lot I never noticed before about drunk folks. Like the invasion of personal space (or my BUBBLE as I call it). And volume. And spit talkers. Crazy. New and exciting stuff for me here, cousins!!!

7. Last, but not least - my brother is my best buddy - and a
    sap! As is his whole family!

> This experience has made me realize (again) how
> sweet big brother Joe is - and the aforementioned
> sap. He was the first I told (besides Neily!) and he
> was very excited and sappy. It was awesome!
> hehehe... Sorry, Joe - I let out your sweet side!!!
> Michelle is excited to have a baby around that she
> gets to cuddle an' love on, but not have to get up for
> late nite feedings and walked floors!   OH, and get
> this - Matthew talked to my belly!!! I'm barely
> showing, but it was the CUTEST thing - he's the
> perfect height to have a conversation with my belly!
> Rob and Gracie are ready to tackle babysitting!!! I'm
> pretty sure there's going to be a few birds n' bees
> questions that I'm happy I don't have to deal with –
> hahaha... I continue to rock the MacLellan boat!!!

Well, dear family - this took me a few days to pen - my focus
and attention are victims of my knocked up state. Love to
you, and hope to drive you drunken fools around soon!

*Various Comments & Ramblings since the above
announcement*

30 weeks

Did I mention I'm a huge pale wonder? Hehehe... I came out of the shower a couple weeks ago crying about soap. Poor Neil was confused until I could explain that we're going thru soap faster because there's more of my glowing white skin to wash. Yeah, I may also have some hormones kicking in too. Hmm...

If I go over 40 weeks - I found this "Eviction Letter" that I plan on posting - I can't find a source for it, but there's versions all over the Internet, so I believe it's not copyrighted or anything.

To: Wee McG

To the above tenant in possession of below described premises:

I am issuing 5-day notice for EVICTION. You will have 5 days in which you can either gather your belongings and promptly vacate the premises, or wait until the final day. After which, you will be physically removed from the property.

You are being evicted due to breech of contract and destruction of property. Expansions only to the FRONT of the house, within reasonable limits, were discussed. Not only have these limits been exceeded, but additions to the back of the house were also made!

Remodeling and gutting of the home was never approved, nor was changing the initial layout and base structure. And due to property damage, there are now leaks in both the upper AND lower levels of the home. On top of which, the landlord has received numerous complaints about nightly disturbances.

After 5 days from this day that you don't comply with the notice will result in immediate and forceful removal at my discretion.

Thank you for your cooperation.

Love,
Mommy

33 Weeks and counting

I'm still shocked that I am pregnant. And although I find myself getting a bit down about the whole "limited fries" diabetes thing, I am happy. I love watching the tumbles going on inside my belly, and love thinking how great a father my husband will make! Then it turns into a serious panic mode, because the next thought after my husband being a father is ME being a mother!!!

Will I be a good mom?
What if I hurt the baby by accidentally rubbing the creepy belly button stump too hard?
What if it's a boy and gets circumcised - I have to TOUCH IT?
What if the baby doesn't like the diapers and bottles we have?
What if the baby gets sick and I don't realize it?
What if the baby gnaws off a nipple? I like having both!
What if the baby stops breathing? I should get baby CPR lessons, but will I remember how to do it?
What if kids at school make fun of my child (after all, dad's a bagpiper and mom's a bookworm/fiddle music lover!)? How much trouble can I get in for tripping a 5-year-old?

And the list goes on and on and spans decades of possible worry. One thing I realized is that I definitely have ADD and miss the medication. At least when medicated, my worry is focused on one or two areas. This is crazy!

I think the fact that my brain is less than focused increases the hormonal reactions I have to things. I know pregnancy causes these hormonal fluctuations, but I think mine are

OVERBOARD because I jump from one type of stimuli to another and take it all in instead of just one at time. I'm like exposed nerves in one's mouth – hot, cold, wet, dry – it all causes a reaction.

For example:

Grocery Shopping – I begin to get tears in my eyes because I want a pineapple. Yes, I know I can eat some, but I want the whole damn thing. Why can't I eat it – diabetes!! So I get bummed out and want to cry. But my diabetic thoughts lead me to when I screwed up the diet and ate a delicious strawberry shortcake. Then a lady walks by with a baby and I can barely hold on... nearly losing it – did I harm my baby by eating that wonderful shortcake? Shit, what about the milkshake two weeks ago? How much have I injured this innocent floating wonder? GET OUT OF PRODUCE!!!

So I leave produce and walk right into... the freakin' bakery. Oh, how I miss bruschetta. Well, I did have some pita that day with Middle Eastern, mmm... it was so good. ACK, but it totally did a number on my blood sugar. Yet, I tried it again, hoping that the meter misread it – nope... high numbers again, and more damage done. I am a horrible mother!!! GET OUT OF THE BAKERY!

I ran past the snack aisle. I feel better because I'm so smart to avoid all sight of Frito Lay chips. I can, and wish to, buy loads of peanuts, but they are flanked by all that potato fried goodness and I can't handle it.

I walk down the frozen food aisle to get some veggies and Lean Cuisines. WHY do they put garlic bread and ice cream right near the low fat foods? Who designed this store? Why is that woman letting her child SCREAM like that? What is wrong with her? What is wrong with me – why am I angry at that lady... kids throw temper tantrums – I was the queen of them! How did that lady get so skinny with a baby that young? Maybe it's not hers, maybe it's the babysitter. CRAP – who's going to watch the baby when I go back to work? Maybe I shouldn't go back to work... but... where was I again? I need ice cream, but NO... RUN...

This all in less than an hour – and then I go home, to increase the chaos of my brain because there's a HUGE range of things to be thought about in my house (from diaper wipes, to closet organizers, to light fixtures, humidifiers, cabinet space, de-deathtrapping my house... etc.). And then my husband chases my chaos away with his simple, wonderfully adept way of addressing each concern with logic... which makes me think of what a great father he'll be... and here I go again!!!!

Moonlight Sonata

Kim Huston

Kim Huston is a piano teacher living in Haslett, Michigan, one of the suburbs that have grown up around Michigan State University. She shares her joy found in piano playing with the many boys and girls whom she instructs. When she gave lessons to my younger son, I was struck with her grace and quiet demeanor, but her love of music is like a fire that glows from within. Something is brought to life in her students because of her. With Kim's blessing, I write about her here.

When I arrive at the community church where the recital is to be held, several people have already arrived. The children, ranging in age from seven to ten, are seated in the front rows. They are unusually quiet as they nervously await their performances. The girls are dressed in skirts and blouses or simple dresses, and the boys have on nice pants, white shirts and ties. It is one of the things I like about Kim Huston. Her attention to detail goes beyond the piano playing to include behavior and dress. In her world there are still good manners.

It is early afternoon, and sunlight streams in through stained glass windows, making soft beams of light in jeweled colors. Felt banners hang from the walls around the altar table, calling us to faith, love, and peace. Several of them display white doves and more beams of light in gold felt. An upright piano is placed in front, a couple of steps above the moms, dads, and grandparents quietly chatting while they wait. I find a seat on the same side as my son Sean, and pour over the little program. Another thing I like about his teacher is the variety of songs she chooses. There are traditional American folk songs; tunes reminiscent of a Spanish flamenco or Russian Cossack; mini-versions of classical pieces; and music that calls to mind the seasons.

Kim has been seeing to a plethora of sweets and snacks for afterwards, and presently comes down the main aisle to get ready to begin. Of medium height, with short strawberry blond hair and ivory skin, she stands before us as mother figure and music maven. It is plain that her students love her, and they breathe a visible sigh of relief as she makes her appearance. Each child is given a brief introduction before they play the two-minute rendition of a song they have practiced for weeks. Everyone receives enthusiastic applause at the end, despite any slip-ups or nervousness. Unlike Simon Cowell's aspiring singers, these kids will all go on to the next round!

Sean was never forced to take lessons, and enjoyed the few years of instruction he received from Ms. Huston in her home. Whenever I dropped him off (and was never invited to stay, probably best), he was absorbed immediately into the family. A girl was at the dining room table doing homework, a dog greeted me and then returned to his nap; but when a student was led to the piano, everyone understood it was quiet time for all but the young person seated in front of the ivories.

At home, Sean practiced faithfully and played his new lessons for me each week. With long fingers given to moving over the keys, he developed a unique style, at turns soft and lyrical, at others vibrant and strong. When my son entered high school and moved on to other activities, we sold our piano to a young family nearby. I was moving to Florida, where my husband and I had a piano. Sean was living with his dad, who eventually inherited one for him to use. In the meantime, his father provided an electronic keyboard (with an appeal all its own!) so, despite all the changes and moves, there was always something available for him to play.

As people drift in and out of our lives, so too did Kim Huston. I thought of her gentle spirit and special spark when I began listing possible invitees for this book. I contacted her via formal letter and she responded with an e-mail. She remembered Sean with affection, and especially recalled "the piano story and how you transferred that piano to other families taking lessons." She also hoped Sean had continued his interest in music.

Ten years later, Kim still teaches young students. She has added to her repertoire of activities, hosting a monthly folk jam of mostly retired folks and adding hammered dulcimer to the instrument she plays so well. She has discovered Praise & Worship music as an accompanist at a church that has a band, and loves the fun of playing in ensembles. But she continues to show a particular fondness for teaching individual students piano lessons at home. In the end, she says no-thank-you to my invitation to write, but agrees that "you could write a piece about my experiences with piano for Sean, and me as his piano teacher. I would not mind at all."

My husband plays beautiful music on the piano, by ear. He can really entertain a crowd. I dabbled in flute as a college student but have always been drawn to piano. One day, while my husband was at a business conference in Arizona, I figured out a system using middle C as "base 1" to play a melody by number, making up chords and background music as I went along. Still, my son gets the prize because he can actually read music!

As of this writing, Sean is a junior at Michigan State University majoring in advertising; snowboarding in winter, playing ultimate Frisbee and life-guarding at Walnut Hills in summer; and "Mr. Sean" to the children he cares for at Haslett Public Schools' latch-key program. He travels as much as he can. He and my husband spend hours fishing when he visits our Florida home. And I enjoy cooking for them when they return. I can fish and my husband can cook, but we fall into traditional roles sometimes, too. Our visits together are full of laughter and a peaceful respite for all three of us.

After dinner, someone usually sits down to play the piano. The sound is like a fingerprint to me. I can tell immediately who is playing by the melodies, the intensity, and the feeling of the music. We all have a style that is individual and rather original. But Sean has the benefit of formal lessons, and Kim Huston to thank for bringing this talent to fruition.

For Christmas of 2009, Sean made us a recording of his performance with the Haslett High School Choirs at Carnegie Hall a few years ago. In conjunction with a couple of other schools and a fabulous orchestra, they sang *Dona Nobis Pacem* by Vaughan Williams, an emotional hour-long Cantata. At the end of the recording there is a pause, and then, the strains of a solo piano piece, "Moonlight Sonata," begin. It is clear that my son has put everything into playing it, as he knows it has meaning as one of our favorites.

Thus, piano is a part of my son that survives the years and emerges as a little escape from the trials and tribulations of his days. And I am always grateful for the joy of learning to play that Kim Huston gave to him. She wonders if Sean has continued his interest in music. How could he not? Like the soft notes of a moonlight sonata, we are drawn to listen, connected by a score on a grand scale, and faith in this song of life.

Quadratic Equation

Kristy Rapley

Kristy Rapley is an ordinary person in most every way. She is bright, attractive, and has a wry sense of humor. She is well-educated, excels at her work for a major oil company, and is an inspiration to many at a local college where she talks to and advises students with disabilities. She and her husband enjoy travel, reading, watching old movies, and going to the horse races. Completely wrapped up in work, she asked me to write something for her. Oh, did I mention that Kristy is a quadriplegic?

It was one of those long, warm, languid nights in the middle of a Midwestern summer, with crickets chirping and barbeque smoke drifting and the moon behind a gauzy curtain of haze. In other words, a perfect night for a pool party. We were all swimming, drinking soft drinks and beer, laughing and talking. Someone started diving through an inner tube in the pool, and I tried it, too. Each dive cooled me off and felt so good and made me want to do it again. On what was to be my last dive, I aimed for the tube and went through easily, but I was too close to the shallow end and my head hit the slope of the concrete bottom with a thud. A thousand tiny needles shot through my body as everything went numb. *I realized I couldn't move.* A short time after I was carried from the pool I heard an ambulance siren, and then the whir of a medivac helicopter.

The aftermath of that night would go on for years, an endless series of treatments and surgeries, physical therapy and psychological trauma, agonies and adjustments. Eventually I had to learn how to live in a wheelchair. I was twenty-five.

Quadriplegia is defined as involvement in four extremities. This can mean weakness or loss of sensation. I learned that my injury was at the C5 and C6 levels of my spine, which meant I could not use my triceps muscle (extend the elbow), my wrist flexor muscles or my hands. I was also left with no use of the trunk (spinal extensors and abdominals), which paraplegics have in some capacity.

The helicopter transported me to the University of Michigan Medical Center where I was stabilized and diagnosed. Next, I was moved to Detroit Receiving Hospital, part of the Detroit Medical Center (DMC), a system of hospitals academically integrated with Wayne State University. Detroit Receiving Hospital is the region's leader in emergency medicine, complex trauma, critical care, neuroscience and gerontology, and it was there that I had my first surgery. Detroit Rehab is part of the Medical Center and offered the area's widest range of rehab services to patients suffering from serious head and neck injuries.

It was there, as I completed nearly a year of out-patient treatment, that I met Bob, the man who would become my husband. He worked at the Center in conjunction with a medical supply company, ensuring ease of transition for the 30 to 40 admissions and 30 to 50 discharges at rehab each day. This involved moving patients, making sure equipment was ready and in good working order, performing basic repairs to wheelchairs, and measuring patients properly for power, manual and shower chairs. Bob's sister was a physical therapist at the hospital, and it was she who introduced us. We did the rest.

Our wedding celebration was held at my parents' home in Richmond, a far northern suburb of Detroit's East Side. The house had been recently purchased, complete with entrance ramps, special shower room, wide doorways and other necessary "conveniences" to accommodate their disabled daughter. My mom proudly showed guests the huge wall quilt of our family tree in the hallway, each member represented by a fabric hand with an embroidered name. She spoke easily of the accident as she showed different changes made to the house. I think it was harder for my dad to express these things and he kept more inside. But they both liked Bob, and they were equally concerned about my happiness, especially on this, our wedding day.

I have never been one to complain much or drown in my sorrows. I'm not big on sentimentality either. I was determined to learn the limitations of what I could and could not do and get on with my life. Quadriplegics develop what is called a *tenodesis* grip. When they extend their wrist the fingers flex and eventually the tendons shorten to allow for a mass grasp. In English, this meant that with a vehicle especially equipped with sensitive hand controls, I could drive again! Like a massive computer game, the van was operated by use of a joystick (actually a three-pronged accelerator and brake on the left and a steering wheel with a similar apparatus on the right) into which I could insert my hand. The wheel and the "joystick" required only a very light touch. If the average person tried to drive the van they would probably flip it or do really bad turns and sudden jolts with the brakes. But it was perfect for me.

The ability to drive meant that I could also work again. But first I had to take specialized driving lessons at Detroit Rehab. Initially, Bob had a brake he could operate from the passenger's seat if I got into trouble, but after a couple of months I really had the hang of it and the extra brake was removed. I applied for and received my driver's license, and have had no tickets or accidents since.

My college studies were in industrial health and safety. Bob was still working with the medical supply company. I had a physical therapist coming to our house in Belleville (just outside of Ann Arbor) on a regular basis, but in the meantime Bob was observing everything and learning how to help—not only with therapy but with my personal hygiene, sleep positions (I had to be turned periodically throughout the night), medications and infection prevention. In addition, he did all of the housework, cooking, laundry (with a specially-equipped, lower-level washer and dryer I threw a load in occasionally but Bob didn't need to know that!) and gardening. We bought a computer. We had acquired a couple of dogs, too: Buddy, a black-and-white border collie, and Bella, a compact white husky. Life wasn't perfect but we were pretty content.

A storm during a chilly Michigan spring day completely changed our lives again. This was only about twelve years ago, but everyone did not have cell phones, On Star, GPS and other personal electronic devices like they do today. Bob had managed to get to work, but I was working in Pontiac at the time, an hour's drive on a good day. Our offices were closed due to the weather. I lived a long way away, and there were still fallen tree limbs and downed power lines to worry about. Since the power was out at home, I decided to go out to the van and get the news, wishing I had a weather-band radio. Riding down the ramp and through the garage, I almost reached the van before my wheelchair became stuck in the mud. It was cool and a steady drizzly rain fell. There were no neighbors close enough to hear me. I sat there all day, helpless until Bob arrived home several hours later.

I remember that he wrapped me in a blanket, carried me inside, and made me a cup of hot chocolate. Then he said, "That's it. This is never going to happen again. We're moving someplace warm." We had been discussing this for some time but now the job hunt began in earnest. Together we pored over the U.S. map and targeted areas of the South and West. With my education and experience, I actually had the better chance of landing a position, and that is exactly what happened. Chevron Oil Corporation contacted me, interviewed me by phone, liked what they heard, checked my credentials, and hired me for a position in air quality technology at their offices in Bakersfield, California. They knew nothing of my disability until I rolled into their offices for the first time.

A new adventure began.

We sold the house in Belleville, an attractive place on a large wooded lot. A moving van came and took most of our belongings. We loaded the rest—including the dogs—in my van and Bob's car, and drove to California. Previously we had flown out, I to complete negotiations with Chevron and Bob to find us a house! The result was that I had a job waiting for me and Bob had a home waiting for us when we arrived.

Bakersfield appears to be in the middle of nowhere, but it is California's third largest inland city. Located at the southern end of the San Joaquin Valley, the economy is supported mainly by agriculture, petroleum extraction and refining, and manufacturing. We loved our house in a new development, close to the office where I would be working. Several handicap-accessible features came with the home, and Bob saw to the rest. There was a large fenced-in yard and a pet entrance so the dogs could come and go freely. Our little family thrived here. With the good weather, nice neighbors, and easier style of living (and the sharp reduction in fast food Bob used to eat on the road), my husband was soon completely off the medicines he had been taking for bad cholesterol. We settled into the routine of our lives.

My new position involved not only air quality and pollutant regulations and compliance, but many work conferences and several regulatory obligations. Bob always came along on any job-related travel, and as my caretaker all expenses were paid for both of us. In this way we were able to see San Diego, San Francisco, Sacramento and Los Angeles. We also took many side trips on our own to see the Pacific Coast, the Redwood forests (big trees and more big trees), the mountains and the desert. California has it all.

It's not always easy. Bob and I are well-matched in many ways but there are some things I can never provide. Once we were invited to a Hawaiian luau to raise money for a community animal rescue group. There were hula dancers performing as part of the evening's entertainment. They noticed Bob sitting next to me in the ol' wheelchair, came down and lured him up on the stage, put leis around his neck and danced around him for a few minutes. The poor guy looked like he was in heaven. As I told my mother-in-law later, "It was an awfully quiet ride home, Mom."

We have lived in Bakersfield for several years now. I have received numerous bonuses and salary increases, and was recently given a promotion when I reached the top of my salary range. There have been a couple of visits home to see family and friends. (Air travel is a whole other odyssey for a quad that I won't bother going into!) The van had a rough ride to California, and had to be replaced and re-equipped for me to drive. Bob made all the trips to Ford, handled the paperwork necessary for federal assistance to pay for it, and went in for all the inspections and approvals needed to purchase my new vehicle. He also bought himself a red Honda Element that accommodates my wheelchair while I sit in the passenger seat, on the rare occasions when we can't use my van.

Buddy and Bella, our constant companions, grew old and died within a few months of each other. We weren't sure we wanted to go through all that again, but in the end we love dogs and have great neighbors who watch out for them when we're away. Recently we adopted two Australian shepherd mixes (brothers) from the shelter, so now Moe and Curly are part of our family. They melt my heart.

Life brings experiences I would never have dreamt of if I hadn't lived through them myself. Sometimes a terrible event can turn into an unimagined blessing. If it weren't for that accident so many years ago, I couldn't possibly have the life I have today!

My Life in Belgium

Laurence Lefebvre

Laurence Lefebvre was at first someone I knew only as the wife of Stéphane DeDeurwaerder, a business associate of my husband. Stéphane had been a guest in our home and we had seen pictures of his family. Laurence always sent Belgian chocolates along as a (welcomed) gift. After many post cards, e-mails, and travel arrangements, we all met at their home for a few days of sheer enjoyment in May of 2010. Laurence is at the same time competent and nurturing, a charming hostess and a wonderful cook. She is devoted to family and passionate about her work. We visited the famous iron atom, symbol of Belgian industry, shown in the picture above. Laurence has an understanding that runs deep and a smile that illuminates the world around her. I was delighted when she agreed to write about her life in Belgium.

My name is Laurence. I live in Belgium in a city of 50,000 inhabitants called Mouscron (*Moo-crohn*).   It is a city of intermediate size with the particular distinction of being divided into a French-speaking section (where we live) along the part that borders France, and a Dutch-speaking section. In fact, all of Belgium is divided this way, so parts of the country have signs and language dominated by the Dutch while the rest is more French. However, the influence of both is found throughout the country.

I have been married to Stéphane for twelve years and we have two wonderful children, a son who is eleven years old and a daughter who is eight. If they are wonderful, it is that we are like all parents, they are wonderful because they are ours. We find ourselves so much through each of our children, who are to some extent the reflection of ourselves, with our assets and our defects. I do not have the impression of living an extraordinary life. I follow my instincts, my desires, and try to have a life that corresponds best with my personality, that reflects the way I have lived and who I am.

After having studied at university in the school of economic sciences and having other professional training and experiences, I work in public administration as General Secretary (administrator). In fact, I lead the institution, in collaboration with a political decision maker; that is to say, an official elected by the people. The institute employs more than five hundred people and provides a wide range of social services: to give aide to the poor, social rehabilitation, daycare, housing for the aged, family services, etc. My work is very enriching because it combines the view of management with the view of the social. Nothing is ever the same at the institution. The unexpected always takes precedence; in return the work is interesting and is my passion. Nevertheless, in working in the service of people with difficulties, I have learned to take a relativistic approach to life. Working with so many people who experience pain in their lives allows me to see things in a much more detached way, more serene, and thus to propose the things that are most important. These important things are simple, close to us.

I was born and grew up in a "normal" family. My current life is simple; I divide myself between my family and my work. The things I find enriching and tremendous are these social connections we can have in life. At age forty I have the good fortune to be close to my husband, whom I love and who, I believe, loves me. Together we form what is known as the modern couple: the art and the science of balancing our lives as much as possible and the education of our children to always respect others.

The children are, of course, students in our town and have the good fortune to go to the home of their maternal grandparents each day after school. This is an opportunity for them to build strong bonds between the generations, giving them direction, essential in life. Their paternal grandparents live near our home but not so close to the school. Still, not a week goes by that we do not visit them. Family ties are vitally important.

To read these lines, there is the impression that everything is wonderful, but there are moments of doubt, thoughts that are present daily. We find that we can always do better; we often feel imperfect. It is difficult to accept that we are not perfect because we would like everything to be just so. But I find it is necessary to accept our personalities, our limits, and our errors in order to grow from them and make ourselves better.

What is a week at my house like?

During the week, after having prepared the satchels (book bags), my husband and I take the children to school, which is located about five kilometers from the house. We each have our own work. My husband is an independent engineer; he has his own company and works in his office next to our home, or with other companies as a consultant. The hours vary and it is difficult to plan a long time in advance what his exact hours will be. It is important to emphasize that in Belgium, business trips are very manageable by car due to the size of the country and our close proximity to other countries. Many business trips are more than 100 kilometers but less than 150 kilometers per day (about 60-90 miles). Living in a small country, it is almost certain Stéphane will return home in the evenings and sleep in his own bed. We are together almost every day to watch over the education of our children and to follow their activities.

Next, I head for my workplace situated less than five km from home. As I mentioned previously, my function as an administrator can result in many unforeseen circumstances, agreeable or not. On any given day I might work at conflict management, urgent housing for people who need shelter, new projects, or a celebration at a convalescent home. In working to find solutions to difficult social problems, I have learned that life can topple (fall apart) very quickly. When people are put to the test, it is so important to know how to rebound, to adapt to new situations, and to keep some hope in the most painful moments. I endeavor to teach these lessons to my children.

To arrive at this goal, I believe they must branch out, with relationships and activities apart from their family and schooling. The young grow by weaving bonds, by engaging in numerous activities that allow them to choose their way, to discover their central area of interest. Nicolas plays the piano (a lesson once a week and practice each day), music theory (two hours per week), basketball (practice twice a week and a match on the weekend), tennis (once a week); Anne-Lise takes piano (same program), music theory (two hours per week), basketball (training on Saturdays), and a tennis course. On Sunday, the children participate in scouting activities, wolf cubs for Nicolas and Goblins (English translation: the Brownies) for Anne-Lise. In this way, they learn how to play and act in nature, to form character, and to respect traditional values toward God, toward others, and toward themselves.

Our weeks are clearly dictated by our work and by looking after the children. That leaves only a little margin for anything else, but we have chosen this life. Sometimes we do enjoy other things (parties, shows, restaurants…) either as a couple or with friends. It is clear that we would like to have more time for cultural and social activities. Work is necessary to make sufficient money in order to live well. Time is precious, and needs to be used intensely and efficiently; this we manage quite happily. We are a family like yours, living in the town of Mouscron, in the country of Belgium.

Freelance Writer on the Treasure Coast

Leona DeRosa Bodie

Vero Beach, Florida — 32963 — is one of the largest book-buying zip codes in the nation. It is a haven for creative writers and a virtual breeding ground for local authors. So it makes perfect sense that I met Leona DeRosa Bodie at the first Vero Beach Book Fair. She was introducing her first children's book. Then I learned she was vice president of the Treasure Coast Writers Guild. Along with that, she thought it would be a good idea to mix literary and fine arts in the area, went to the City, and ended up serving as chair for Authors and Artists, a showcase for the many people who needed a venue to network and sell their wares. Recently Leona published her first adult fiction, a thriller called Shadow Cay. *Who knows what she'll come up with next?*

My career took me from high school English teacher to a biotechnology corporate executive and former president of the Greater Miami Society of Human Resource Management before I shifted to writing books. Today I'm the author of a new suspense novel, *Shadow Cay*, and four illustrated children's books. Besides working on another novel, I'm a freelance writer and editor, vice president of the Treasure Coast Writers Guild, and a local group leader for the Florida Writers Association. I live with my husband Walter, a former Miami-Dade forensic specialist, on the Treasure Coast of Florida. Our two grown sons live nearby.

Over the years, writing has been my passion and release. Though at times it's been a challenge finding time for everything, including raising a family in a dynamic city, working full-time, re-engineering my career, taking care of aged parents and simultaneously building our home—from scratch, I might add. That's right! We laid concrete foundations, erected cinder blocks, applied stucco, and learned to do electrical work and plumbing from Time/Life Books, while our youngest played in a playpen beside us.

For me, reading is a passion that starts the moment I share a book with a child. Growing up, my four siblings and I had a house full of books, from novels to encyclopedias. I credit my mom with instilling a love of reading in me. Her native tongue was Portuguese, and she didn't learn to speak English until she was seven. What I didn't know until I became a teenager was that my father was illiterate. When I saw how well he could hide his personal challenge, I understood the clues, and brought them with me to the classroom as an English teacher.

As the oldest of five and having won two scholarships, I'm the first person in my family to attend college. Paving the way for the others, I've been fortunate to see my brother and sisters earn the same distinction. I earned a bachelor's degree with dual majors in English and Education from Fairleigh Dickinson University. After attaining the distinction of Who's Who Among

Students at American Colleges & Universities, I set out to achieve similar milestones in the workforce.

I have a lifetime certification as senior professional from the Society of Human Resource Management. In 1998 I was awarded the South Florida Best Practices Award for Motivating and Retaining Employees for a Miami software development company. The following year, the Greater Miami chapter, representing 400 employers in South Florida, recognized me for the Excellence in Achievement Award.

In August 2000 I successfully completed the Writer's Digest School's Novel Writing Workshop, and in January 2004 won The Stuart News/Scripps News Second Annual Writing Contest by creating a recurring hero in a fictitious series of crime/mystery novels. More recently, I won *Byline Magazine's* Short-Short Story, Short-Article, and Character Sketch Honorable Mention Awards in 2005 and 2006.

Today I enjoy visiting local schools with my "Meet the Author" presentation, and describe myself as a "bookpreneur," since I also create custom gift baskets, designed a clothing line, and built a website focusing on childhood literacy and educational activities. Parents want to give their children a brighter future, and families who introduce infants and toddlers to books give them a head start in school — and in life.

After a career in human resources in Miami, and as a high school English teacher in Runnemede, N.J., I began freelance writing and venturing into suspense fiction. However, after enjoying watching grandson Logan grow from baby to toddler, I got an idea for a solidly-constructed book with cheerful illustrations about tots.

My husband did the cover and interior layout; my illustrator, Catherine Baptista Davis, is my 85-year-old mother, a watercolorist with a passion for seascapes and lighthouses, and a professional artist since 1998. My mother started painting when she was 75, like Grandma Moses. And I wanted to write new classics with an old-fashioned appeal to encourage every child. It's been a labor of love, because so many family members got involved.

The result is the 32-page board book *One is Fun* (Ages 0-4). It was assigned to a pre-selected group of kids by a panel of judges including child psychologists, child educators and parents. They monitored the children and evaluated the book based on four major factors: educational value, creative nurturing, creative play and overall value with respect to retail price. Upon completion of the assessment, *One is Fun* was awarded Creative Child Magazine's prestigious Preferred Choice Award.

My second book, *Skating for Two* (Ages 3-10) is a tale about first-time experiences, told in the style of a Dr. Seuss prose poem. It encourages children to overcome obstacles and teaches the merits of good deeds. Kids love kind, purposeful Leah and cheer her overcoming fears. Whimsical illustrations and witty rhymes keep preschoolers up to grade 4 captivated. As an added bonus, the book includes a reading guide, lesson plans, fluency fun and a vocabulary list. Both books are sweet stories with great messages for kids. They stress learning is fun at any age and promote joy in family interactions.

Despite a string of successes with my kids' books, I hankered to take a detour. My dream for the past fifteen years was to write a mainstream suspense novel, and it came true in

April 2010 with the launch of *Shadow Cay*. I wrote the lead character with Johnny Depp in mind. With its cinematic flair, hopefully the book that's currently with a Hollywood movie producer will be major motion picture! Miami and the Bahamian Out Islands are prominently featured in this instant-hook thriller.

Shadow Cay is a story I *had* to write. Many things influenced me on this journey, including our travels, my husband's forensic expertise, my biotech experiences and his. Even the current Middle East wars, the current economic times, and the business downturn factored into my plotline. On the dark side of American industry, there is no more precious commodity than money. Sometimes lackluster financial statements, pessimistic stakeholders and global competition fuel greed and inhumanity. But what happens to those who openly oppose the new order with its radically different interpretations of corporate progress? When industry icons sell their soul, ethical employees become huge liabilities. Pack these elements into a go-fast boat, and you have a wild ride through the *Floribbean*. That's SHADOW CAY!

I'm not sure which was more enjoyable: writing the book or researching it. Half of the story takes place in the Bahamian Out Islands. For three months my husband and I cruised approximately 1,700 miles of this area in our 34-foot sailboat, *Chasing Clouds*. During this adventure I read Bahamian history books, saw and photographed the sights, and talked with local experts. Our itinerary ranged from the usual tourist traps to remote, uninhabited islets in the heart of the Bermuda Triangle, miles from the typical traveler's radar. Here, we enjoyed crystalline water, unspoiled white beaches and surreal sunsets.

I wrote most of *Shadow Cay* on our sailboat, surrounded by these incredible views. And the show stopper was Normans Cay. My research into its history led me to flash back two decades: A dramatic flying adventure, international intrigue, a forced crash landing, a brush with death, and a tropical island paradise with a seedy secret.

The other half of the story takes place in Miami, where I lived for twenty-seven years. As the wife of a forensic professional with twenty-one years in the Miami Dade Police Department (MDPD) crime lab, I quickly absorbed Miami's underbelly and the critical role forensics plays in solving crimes. Thanks to my husband Walt's expertise, I also have a ready resource and a technical advisor who always answers my endless questions about police and lab procedurals.

The fact that other people are talking about my debut novel is heady stuff. This week it was endorsed by the President of the Florida Association of Forensic Professionals (FAOFP)! Chere Reynolds, Criminalist II, MDPD and the President of FAOFP said, "Leona Bodie is a masterful storyteller, and I highly recommend her new thriller, *Shadow Cay*. The MDPD Crime Lab was inspiration for some parts of her first novel. This book speaks to the challenges Forensic Professionals face every day. *Shadow Cay* is a steamy suspense about murder, a drug cartel and corruption taking place in the tropics between Miami and the Bahamas."

Award-winning author Malcolm Mahr said, "*Shadow Cay* is filled with dark secrets and gripping suspense. Leona Bodie clearly has intimate knowledge of the Bahamas and the profession of 'forensic science' that encompasses more than the cops, fingerprints, and DNA analyses found in most whodunits."

I love writing and would do it without the praise, but it certainly adds the umbrella to my tropical cocktail!

A Villa in Italy

Linda Lovisa

In October of 2009, Linda Lovisa was a guest at a wedding I attended on Salt Spring Island, just off the coast of Victoria, British Columbia. She made the trip alone, so my husband and I invited her to spend a free day with us. We visited island art studios, perused a bookstore and had lunch at a restaurant on the harbor. Linda is an accountant by trade, interesting by any standard. She is a well-traveled soul, gentle in demeanor and just plain nice. I couldn't get her story about the family villa in Italy out of my mind. We kept in touch, and I was pleased when she agreed to write about it.

I remember it as if it were yesterday. The long flight and then the five-hour car ride from Milan. During the overnight flight my 11-month-old daughter slept blessedly in a makeshift bed on the floor in the bulkhead row. The car ride after offered her a goofy "car seat" they supplied in Milan: a round wooden piece with a metal ring to hold her upright as her legs were slipped through the rungs. And then, the miles and miles of rice paddies we passed by in northern Italy—who knew it was a huge rice growing area? Finally, arriving at our destination, the first time for me, was heaven. I was glad I was traveling with my in-laws. Beth and I were staying for five weeks, and her dad would join us for three weeks in the middle. I didn't speak much Italian back then, smiled a lot and relied on my mother-in-law or husband to know what was going on.

This was my husband's grandfather's house, located in the northeastern tip of the Italian boot, Cavasso Nuovo to be exact. Cavasso Nuovo is in the province of Pordenone, an area settled before 1000 A.D., a thriving river port and a center of commerce and trade from the 12th to the 19th century. Napoleon gave Pordenone to the Austrian Empire in 1797, and it remained so until 1866 when it was annexed to the Reign of Italy.* Only 1,500 people inhabit Cavasso Nuovo, and the second most common surname is mine: *Lovisa*.

The villa has been a true treasure in our lives as we have raised our family, a family home to visit in northern Italy during the summers. My husband's grandparents were always there as they spent the entire summer over there. Time spent at the villa often included aunts, uncles, cousins, their kids, and now a new generation of little ones coming along. My in-laws, the children's grandparents, were also there, as they, too, spent the season in Italy. We would drop in for two or three weeks, bringing lots of noise, confusion and family fun to their otherwise tranquil place. So many summers, so many memories.

The first year a small crib, borrowed from some relative, was waiting in our bedroom when we arrived. The large metal tub used to wash the clothes was quickly replaced by a proper, albeit very small, washing machine. The tub gained a second life as the perfect size "swimming pool" for a toddler. Although we arrived with an infant, she took her first steps on the Italian porch. I was not there at the time — my husband, Van, and I had left Beth in Grandma's superb care and gone for a day trip to nearby Venice with his cousins — and Grandma never let me forget it!

And, the food! Friuli, the area where my husband is from, is known as "Italy's secret garden" according to famous food writer, Fred Plotkin. Love and respect for food are described as the pride and banner of this region, which combines the freshness of Mediterranean cuisine, the mountain goodness of Alpine dishes, and the savory flavors of Austro-Hungarian specialties. Simple ingredients, fresh and delicious. Polenta with everything. With the famous prosciutto factories of San Daniele just down the road, we could never get tired of eating this sweet delicacy. San Daniele prosciutto is made by only twenty-seven small producers within the town of San Daniele. According to the locals, it is the quality of the pigs, the fresh air from the nearby Alps, the humidity of the Adriatic, and the simple seasoning (sea salt, no additives) that makes prosciutto ham from this region such a treat.

That first trip was so wonderful, both an introduction to Friuli and a chance for Beth to spend loads of time with her grandparents. Hanging out with Nonno and Nonna has always been one of the better aspects of our frequent return visits to Italy over the years. Nonno doesn't speak much English, having immigrated to the U.S.A. as a grown man and having always worked with Italians in the tile and terrazzo business. Stone and tile workers were Friuli's main export after World War II. The area, so prosperous now, was very poor after the war and work was scarce. My husband was just two years old when his parents came to the U.S., having been born in this very house! But Nonno, with his limited English, knew exactly how to communicate with his grandchildren—a smile, down on all fours, a goofy stuffed animal in his hand—that's all he needed and they loved him so.

It would be a few years after that first trip before we could return. Another baby the following summer, so we waited until he was three, and then off we went. That year and every year after that until the next one came along. Short break, then continuing the tradition, by now showing up as a family of five! First one, then two, finally three small children's beds appeared over the years, and a bigger refrigerator. The washtub was replaced with a proper blow-up kiddie pool. Legos, cars, coloring books, dolls, all appeared; and no trip to the Monday Market with Nonno was complete until each child had a toy to bring home.

We were on vacation and nobody (me) wanted to cook all the time, so off to restaurants for lunch. Easy to do in Italy where they are delighted to see you arrive with, one, two, even three children. After the pasta course, the kids would play cards while the adults finished eating and talking. These were the years before cell phones and tri-band, so dad really got a *break* from the office. Once a week he would go to the bar in the piazza and use a pay phone to check in, the phone counting the time with a little attached meter. One year we rented a cell phone; it had to come from the UK to work in Europe and was the size of my shoe!

We discovered the nearby tennis courts, and soon the two oldest children were advanced enough to play doubles with us. It wasn't long until the "kids," by this time teens, were consistently beating the parents—thanks to all those tennis lessons at home. So that became the routine: tennis in the morning before it got too hot, freshen up for lunch at any one of our dozen favorite restaurants, then home for a rest and work on the crossword. Amazing how cool a house will remain when the walls are made of stone and over a foot thick. Then off to the river for a quick swim in the icy waters coming down out of the Dolomites. Visits to various aunts, cousins, and a modest dinner at home. Dad and the two oldest kids developed a special card game, Mom served up some snacks. No TV or Internet yet, so truly a relaxing, family-oriented time. This routine lasted until Beth, our infant on the first trip, graduated from college. Of course, we have laptops now—still no Internet—but we all crowd around to watch a DVD. Young adults always know all the funniest movies.

The villa in Italy now belongs to us. We love this place as a family getaway, cherish the times spent with relatives who have gone before us, and look forward to new memories with generations to come. Everyone should have a place where they can forget their troubles, spend time together, and enjoy the simple pleasures of life. For us, that place is Cavasso Nuovo.

Reign of Italy: The history of Italy dates back to the Etruscans and is marked by centuries of divisions and discord. In 1278 the feudal state of Pordenone passed to the Hapsburgs and became an Austrian enclave. In 1514 it was acquired by the Republic of Venice. Pordenone later came under Austrian rule once again when it surrendered to Napoleon. After Napoleon's fall, the city, along with the rest of Friuli and Veneto, were added to the Lombard-Venetian Reign founded by Austria with the Treaty of Vienna. Finally, in 1866 it was annexed to Italy and became part of the Italian Reign.

My Dear Jack
Lynda Tissington

Lynda Tissington is the quintessential British woman, embodied in classic clothing, generosity of spirit, easy wit, a bit of gardening and needlepoint, and that lovely accent. She enjoyed a career as a registered nurse. Born in England, she has lived for many years in the Bushmills area of Northern Ireland, a ten-minute walk from the sea that separates her from her original home. Lynda and her beloved husband, Jack, raised a son and three daughters who now make their homes on three continents. Still, they retain a remarkable family closeness and ease with one another I couldn't help but envy. Devastated when Jack became ill and recently passed away, she offered to write a love letter to him. Knowing what a love they shared and missing this old friend myself, I readily agreed.

Bushmills
Northern Ireland

My Dear Jack,

I can hardly believe that it is nearly two years since you first started to feel unwell. First of all it was just tiredness with some weight loss (you were overweight anyway so that wasn't a problem!) Later your mobility became poor and you began to lack concentration. Tests, however, proved negative, even the MRI scan of your brain. It was a real mystery, wasn't it?

When, after a further spell in hospital, a diagnosis of inoperable brain tumour was given (although I never told you), I took you home to nurse you myself. For a year or more I stayed in with you, you sitting in your big chair by the window, me sitting close to you holding your hand, always holding your hand whenever you were awake and sometimes when you slept. I would put my head on the pillow when you rested your head so we'd feel close, remember?

To stimulate you, I'd read you the newspaper, cover to cover; then we'd watch soccer or cricket on TV, and I even gave in to a black and white cowboy movie now and then because I knew you loved them so.

And I talked and talked to keep you awake. I always was a chatterbox, wasn't I? You were the quiet one! Now you had no option but to listen to me! Mind you, I know you always enjoyed all the reminiscing I did for you; after all, we'd known each other for sixty years and been married for nearly fifty. So we had lots of memories of family times, holidays, travel; and oh, what a lot of fun we had, didn't we? We shared much laughter in our life and a wonderful family and friends. I went on and on every day, sometimes repeating things in case you hadn't remembered from the previous day.

Our four children, spouses and grandchildren are scattered in America, England, here in Ireland, and Australia, but they all came to see you as often as they could. Your face always lit up as they bounced in through the door. They brought laughter into the house, saving the tears for the night time. Remember the girls standing by your bed singing "If you call out my name, I'll come running..."?

You were loved so much Jack, by all the family. There was always a count of sixteen of us, wasn't there? Children, spouses and grandchildren.

When our son decided to get married in Australia we were so sad we couldn't be there for him. We looked at the photos on our computer and were glad for them as they looked so happy. They decided to come over to Ireland for their honeymoon and have a celebratory wedding dinner at a nearby hotel for all the family and some close friends. I wasn't too sure, as by then you had been admitted to hospital, and I was very worried in case you passed before everyone got here or even after they had all left to go home.

I talked to you about their plans and you nodded in agreement that they should go ahead. You always so enjoyed a party, didn't you, love? Pity you and I didn't get there! Anyway, all the preparation took their minds off the sad time we'd been having. The girls e-mailed back and forth arranging hotel, flowers, photographer, menu, etc. Our granddaughters bought new dresses, and our grandsons agreed to discard T-shirts and jeans for shirts and ties! I have lovely photos of them all, but sadly you never got to see them.

Everyone arrived a few days beforehand so were able to see you, a few at a time, holding your now nearly worn-out hand and talking to you, telling you all their news. Yes, you knew them all, and I reminded you that for the first time in three years all sixteen of us were together. You smiled at that, didn't you?

Came the day of the celebration, you had taken a turn for the worse. You had slipped into a semi-conscious state and were sleeping peacefully when we all came to see you. I insisted they carry on as I knew you would have wanted, and they reluctantly went to the party, not really knowing how near the end you were.

I sat by your bed and talked you through the celebration party: "Now they will be on the entrée, now the dessert, now our son will be giving his speech, now our daughters their poems." I said to you, "Aren't we so lucky, Jack, to have all our wonderful family together?" Then I told you it was time for you to go, and you very peacefully passed away.

Jack, my darling, all your life you were a good timekeeper, never late for meetings or any appointments, and now out of 365 days you chose the perfect time of a unique day, when all sixteen of us were near, to leave this world!

They were also there to be at your funeral, where our son gave a beautiful eulogy and our granddaughters wrote a poem to you. You would have been so proud. All your friends came to give you a good send-off. You were a well-loved man!

Oh, and by the way, did you think we were down to fifteen now that you are gone? Well, you are so wrong, as our new granddaughter was born two weeks ago in Australia, so now we are sixteen again.

My dear Jack, thank you for our family and all you have given to me over the years. We've had our ups and downs like most people, but love has conquered all.

Yours always,
Lyn

My American Fairy Tale

Lyne Hebig

Lyne Hebig is a lovely French-Canadian American with a soft voice that belies a certain strength beneath. She is bright, perceptive, cheerful and loving, with the perfect dash of the fiery French spirit. I first met her when she was vacationing with her family in Vero Beach. Again, we met in Vero when she traveled from her home in Plano, Texas, for a family reunion at the storybook Disney Resort here. Coincidentally, a space shuttle launch was scheduled for that night and we drank champagne and watched from the beach in awe. Fairy tales and fireworks: the perfect words to describe Lyne.

Do you ever wonder what would have happened if the prince hadn't found the shoe in *Cinderella*? If Aladdin had never found the genie's lamp? Or if Jack had failed to trade the cow for some magic beans? We all know there would have been some sad endings to these beloved fairy tales; and bedtime storytelling wouldn't be as happy for the millions of children who delight in these stories every night. Well, my own fairy tale started pretty much the same way—quite unexpectedly and with a chance encounter.

It was with a dear girlfriend by my side and a backpack full of shorts and T-shirts on my shoulders that I took an Alitalia flight from Montreal, Canada to Rome, Italy in July 1982, a couple of weeks short of my 20th birthday. And it was on this magical trip that I met my prince charming, Jeff, and began what would be my very own fairy tale: "Once Upon a time...a French Canadian college student would travel all the way to Italy to meet an American Naval Officer... "

Fast forward twenty-seven years and I find myself still married to my Prince Charming and the proud mom of three Little Bo Peeps (13, 16 and 17 years old — actually the 17-year-old is not so little!). And I'm happy to report that not all fairy tales take place in The Enchanted Forest. After a FIRST wedding in 1986 (in the U.S.A. in front of a JP) and a SECOND wedding in 1988, this one in Canada with family and friends, our lives have taken us from Washington, D.C. to New York City to Boston to Connecticut to Wichita, KS (don't ask) and finally to Dallas, TX, where we have lived now for fifteen years. Who needs a magic carpet?

So how has the transition been for a French-speaking girl transplanted into American customs and traditions? Surprisingly smooth. After all these years, I couldn't see myself living any other place. I have learned some wonderful new traditions while being free to keep some of my own. Adopting some of these new ways came easy and have become quite dear to me, like eating burgers and corn on the cob on Fourth of July. Enjoying the endless fields of bluebonnets while driving on Texas highways in April. Delighting in warm pretzels covered with bright yellow mustard at a baseball game. Learning the inspiring lyrics to "The Star Spangled Banner." These are only a few of the traditions that have become engrained in the tapestry of my life on American soil.

As expected, other things definitely have required some getting used to. The big adjustments would include being away from my parents and two brothers. Even if we get to see each other a few times per year, I miss being able to share the more mundane events with them like school recitals, backyard barbecues, our kids' hockey and basketball games. I also miss speaking French more often. Thankfully, the satellite radio in my car has become my lifeline to what goes on in Montreal and Quebec City. Even if I'm 1500 miles away, I get the chance to listen to the favorite French songs I grew up with. While listening to that satellite station, I can also imagine the delight on kids' faces when hearing the weather forecast calling for a big snow storm. It all brings back such great memories. In keeping with my heritage, I also enjoy the special bond I have developed with the two French teachers of my high school children. Being able to speak the language and use expressions that only French-speaking people can fully understand has made us become instant friends.

Other adjustments were smaller but nonetheless have been somehow interesting. To this day, I am still learning the traditions surrounding Texas's second religion: football. I remember my gasp when our son showed me the mum he was about to present to his date for his high school's homecoming game. I couldn't believe the size of the "thing." I can honestly say that there was enough ribbon on it to wrap Christmas presents for a family of eight! Another challenge has been the pronunciation of the letter *h*. We never pronounce the letter *h* in French. As a result, the names Hallie, Hannah and the like continue to be mispronounced, much to the frustration of my daughter Kaitlyn. "Mom, it's not Allie, it's HALLIE!"

Thanks to my French upbringing, cooking has always been an integral part of what defines me as a person. Many of the things my American husband and children had to get used to due to my heritage revolve around food: *bûche de Noël* at Christmastime, *boeuf bourguignon* (a glorified beef stew using a full bottle of red wine) in winter months, delicate cheeses at lunchtime, sliver-thin crepes for breakfast, *mousse au chocolat* for a decadent dessert. Regardless of the hectic pace of our family, I strive to serve homemade meals every weeknight. People tend to be at home more often in Quebec than they do here and I find that sad. Our family gets such enjoyment from eating meals together and my kids have developed quite sophisticated palates as a bonus. My cooking is a blend of French, American and some Tex-Mex thrown in. I put emphasis on choosing healthy ingredients, and because of that a dear friend of ours has labeled me "The Food Evangelist." Yes, I do try to convert everyone around me into making better food choices. I am now very familiar with American cuisine but I still don't understand such things as sweet potatoes with marshmallows. How bizarre...but on the other hand, I have grown absolutely crazy about PB&J sandwiches, a total unknown in French culture. They really don't know what they're missing!

One of the best things about living in the United States has been the opportunity of celebrating Thanksgiving. It has become, by far, my favorite holiday and one that I look forward to celebrating again as soon as the last of the pumpkin pie has been eaten. My French-speaking parents come to celebrate Thanksgiving with us every November and it has become their favorite holiday as well. Over the years I've been able to develop my own traditions and recipes for this special day.

I have always felt welcome in this country, and have enjoyed the opportunity of mixing my native and adopted cultures. There is not a day that goes by when I don't feel blessed to be living my fairy tale on American soil.

Leave it to Cupid

Marianne Heimerl-Montague

Marianne Heimerl-Montague was born in Germany, reared in Switzerland, worked for Air France, and has lived many years in America. She is currently engaged to an Irishman who may secure a job with NATO. This would result in a return to Germany, where it all began. The NATO job turned out to be too long of a commitment; however, there may be something in Beijing. But first, Marianne has a few sexy, scandalous experiences to relate. Like a German Jeanne d'Arc, I would call her a Soldier of Love, but she would probably prefer Valentine as her patron saint. Eros is definitely her muse.

I feel so young and light in the arms of my new love. My desires run lusciously uninhibited…

I feel his athletic body awakening all my senses and shiver in anticipation. I want to make this exquisite feeling last. I hold my breath to stretch out every precious moment of intimate touching. Every long kiss makes my breasts tingle, as if motherhood could still be a consequence of this event. Every caress is another ecstatic little step toward fulfillment.

Finally, I can neither think nor speak…

When reasoning returns, I am certain I have found my final love, my soulmate, the true until-death-do-us-part. My man with whom I can still conquer the world.

Oh — thank you, crazy, capricious little Cupid!

Romantic love scenes as just described unfold all over the world multiple times per second and mine would not be notable whatsoever, if it were not for the fact that I am a 62-year-old woman. To make this episode even more noteworthy, I emphasize that I had been crushed and devastated by relationships three times before during my life. Accordingly, several times over three decades I swore indifference to any higher power that would tempt me again into amorous ventures. For years at a time I was determined to avoid personal bonds with anything masculine, except perhaps with a small male pet.

Yet, Cupid, our pudgy little God of love and beauty, son of Venus and Mercury, never abandoned me. During my happy times he let me go my own way and fluttered around to pursue others. Alternately, during my periods of loneliness he outright stalked me. No matter how much I tried to avoid him, this enchanting creature of legends aimed his love arrows straight at my heart four times in my life. All his arrows hit hard, right in the center, and every time they bestowed passion and happiness on me again.

Here's my story:

When I was in my twenties, never in my wildest dreams would I have envisioned such tender and erotic moments in the sixth decade of my life. As a matter of fact, I would have laughed out loud if anyone had described this scenario to me. After a hearty giggle I would have dismissed the thought as completely ridiculous, maybe even somewhat nauseating.

My twenties seemed so certain to deliver love and a suitable husband, optimistically for much longer than just into my sixties. I didn't take the task of finding the right suitor lightly. I wasn't just focused; I was practically consumed with the search for a good man with whom I could live happily ever after.

Since my youth lacked the privileges of being born into a society of debutante balls, I chose a job that promised contacts with the opposite sex. As a flight attendant for Pan Am, I was showered with opportunities to explore the possibilities. Cruising 30,000 feet above the oceans for four years produced more propositions for dates than most young women can find in today's Internet dating age. I envision that Cupid screened each new arriving passenger load diligently for possibilities.

One night in 1972 in a crowded 747 to Rome, Cupid aimed at my heart for the first time. His arrow struck with full force. Suddenly, I became acutely aware of the presence of one passenger, Michael. An overwhelming desire overcame me to touch his tanned hands. I didn't, yet. But four hours later while I handed him the second drink I gave in to my awareness and let his fingers touch mine. I knew that something special had happened. Michael was sensitive and smart. He also had the bluest eyes, beautiful dark hair, and he was of Italian descent. I called him my "sunny boy."

We married in 1972. Our existence was joyous and light. In 1973 I became a very happy mother to my son Robert. Bliss ruled our small household in Montauk. Michael's cheerfulness was contagious and there was no space for arguments in our household. It seemed I had reached my life's goals: the loving husband, the baby, the house...

Unfortunately, Cupid's competencies do not cover the outcome of his matchmaking ventures. Once his arrow hits, his job is done. Other forces take over. And so the unimaginable happened to me. In 1980 I found myself alone again—divorced, devastated, and disillusioned. Michael had left me and his young son to join the cult of Scientology. They absorbed his body and soul. He was gone.

The early 1980s were a time of bitterness and hard work. I had to provide for my son. At the same time I worked on completing my bachelor's degree. Every day was a new painful exercise in functioning at the brink of exhaustion. My sweet little boy did not fully understand that his dad had left him for good. He was just a little guy in elementary school and he already felt the pressures of having to behave manly. He used to say, "Mom, stop crying, don't worry, I'll take care of you." Night after night I cried my eyes out. I was overcome by sadness because Robert had lost his dad and it touched me so deeply that my boy wanted to console me.

As I struggled along, Cupid must have been advised that a new job was waiting for him. A re-do, so to say. I imagine him with frowns on his rounded forehead pondering what had gone wrong the first time and how to get better results this time. He must have been appalled to note that I had only sarcastic and contemptuous ideas about men. My son was my only great love.

I can only visualize the relief in Cupid's mind when he noted that, at least, I kept up a few friendships with women. I found it occasionally refreshing to spend time with a person who shared my own substandard outlook on men. One Saturday evening my colleague Nancy, a bubbly, divorced blonde with two children, persuaded me to visit Stan's on Las Olas in Fort Lauderdale.

At Stan's I enjoyed watching white boats passing on the illuminated Intracoastal Waterway. The large silk trees by the dance floor carried golden light decorations. Their warm glow was captivating. The saucy decorations around the bar and dance floor were all designed to seduce the guests into a romantic mode. I hummed to the smooth sounds of the band. The singer was a pretty redhead with a good, dark voice. The vocal theme was the Sixties—such a "Strangers in the Night," "Monday, Monday" mood. I sipped something that tasted tangy and delicious. Then I felt a wonderful little buzz; sooo relaxing. I felt at EASE. That's when Cupid in his heavenly operations center must have noted that I was in a receptive mood. A pleasant looking grey-haired man politely guided my friend away to the dance floor. I pondered something silly, like whether blondes have more fun...

Someone gently tapped my right shoulder from behind. I started a bit. Would I like to dance? Sure. Cupid put his arrow into ready position, aiming painstakingly. As my steps harmonized with the man's to a slow foxtrot, a sharp Cupid-arrow pierced my heart gently and sweetly. Suddenly I became pleasantly aware of the closeness of this stranger's body. What a wonderful manly voice he had. A whiff of aftershave or cologne woke up my senses. His face was close to mine. A quick glance into his blue eyes and at his masculine features made me like him. I didn't talk much because just moving together to the dance rhythm felt so arousing. We danced silently, as couples do when they have known each other for a long time. To make up for the lack of verbal contact I snuggled closer to his chest. The band played non-stop. Cupid must have chuckled contentedly before he left Stan's. That evening Charles and I danced into the morning hours. We married in July of 1982.

Charles was a retired Air Force pilot who had suffered a minor crash during one landing. His chronic back pain caused me to become an expert in lumbar backrubs. Over time the love for my new husband grew immensely. Our little family of three worked well. Robert was nine years old and hung on to every one of his new stepfather's words. Charles even succeeded in teaching Robert swimming, a project on which I had given up.

I was successful in my work and earned various promotions. This was a direct consequence of not having to worry about Robert's well-being all by myself any longer. I passed the CPA examination, which resulted in more promotions. Our spousal love for each other continued to grow passionately. Most weekends were spent with family activities during the day and with candlelight dinners in the evening. Lovemaking was tender and unforgettable.

Our happy phase lasted for about five years. By that time Robert had grown into a teenager. Charles had kept his promise to care for him as for his own son. But in 1987 something happened, which, to this day, I cannot comprehend. Charles began to insist stubbornly that Robert be sent off to a military school in another state. Purpose: to transform Robert into a more disciplined version of himself and into a good football player.

To understand my consternation and bewilderment about Charles' intentions, I need to explain to my reader that my son certainly was no angel; but he never, ever lacked respect for his stepfather. Why did Charles want to send him away? In general Robert did not give anybody a hard time; he was not a difficult child in his early teens. Also, Robert was not at all a sporty type of kid. Robert's idea of a good time was stuffing his face at Chuckee Cheese, and not at all working up a sweat on a football field. Charles' obsession with the idea to make our pudgy, physically rather inert Robert into a disciplined sports ace and an agile part of the U.S. military seemed ridiculous and alarming to me.

Initially I hoped this eccentric requirement would be temporary. It was not. Verbal disputes over military school and football soon became painful daily occurrences. They ripped into our marriage like tornadoes and left our feelings in shreds. Over the time of about six months we became more and more silent with each other, until conversation ceased forever. Instead, Charles started to smoke and drink again.

I sought out marital counseling, youth counseling for Robert, personal counseling for Charles and myself separately, group counseling, and weekend marriage-repair workshops. I even talked to the parish priest. Nothing helped us. Living together became unbearable. In September 1988 I filed for divorce. Robert said to me, unforgettably, "Mom, don't do that because you'll feel so ALONE!" But the marriage was sprung. From my point of view I had been forced to choose between keeping a husband *or* a son. I chose my son.

Without custody hassles or property division, the divorce was granted quickly. I left with just my clothes and few personal belongings. Charles passed away from a sudden heart failure six days after the divorce was granted. To this day the marriage to Charles makes me feel like his widow, not a divorcee.

When Charles died, my will to live subsided. I staggered through the daily routines, but my emotions were shifting between being numb and inconsolably sad. My sadness was so profound that I envied the dead.

Unenthusiastically I bought a small house for Robert and me in Boca. I got up early every morning to fulfill my work duties as a controller for the bank. Robert stayed alone at the house during long afternoon hours. I couldn't change that; I had to work to pay the mortgage and bring food to the table. Robert was fifteen years old. How often did I remember his words: "... Mom, you'll be so alone!"

During the nights I tortured myself with second-guessing. Had I done it all wrong? Would Robert not have been better off in military school than in the unsupervised situation I left him now every afternoon? To pour salt into my wound, Robert started to smoke. He brought home shady friends. He finally dropped out of high school. Night after night I cried in despair. Soon I was convinced that I had done everything, absolutely everything, wrong. I had reached the abyss of my life and felt that dying would be a relief.

But life continued ruthlessly. The year 1989 greeted me as a single working mother for the second time in my life. I had to prepare breakfasts, argue with Robert about not going to school, and perform competently in my job. Instead of returning to high school, Robert took a job in an ice cream parlor. One day, after a few exceptionally nasty customers had harried him, he asked me whether he could enroll in vocational school. Of course! Next day I stood in the enrollment line for him. When I handed him the school papers, his face lit up with a wide grin. For the first time in many months I felt, deep inside, barely detectable, a faint glimmer of joy.

Time heals all wounds. It's really true. My son and I eventually fell into a productive daily routine. Life offered no happiness worth mentioning, but at least order had returned and our existence had again become manageable. This was probably the time when Cupid received his third work-order for me: yet *another* re-do for me, the difficult case.

My social activities were kept to a minimum and carried out mainly among colleagues. Every year the bank arranged a Christmas party at Pete's in Boca. For that occasion I applied a little more makeup than usual. It's bizarre what a few specks of mascara and eyeliner can do for a woman's spirit. I felt adventurous as I sailed through the restaurant toward our party of about sixty people. At least one man in the room traced my heightened mood. He sensed availability, even though I felt only contentment. He appeared to be sitting at the bar all by himself, nursing a drink. However, my attentive Cupid must have lingered close by, laying out his strategy.

I didn't know it at the time, but the man at the bar observed me during our entire animated party. After witty small presents and merry Christmas wishes had been exchanged, I gathered my belongings to go home. By now Cupid was fully prepared. As I walked to the restaurant's exit door the man at the bar purposefully dropped his wallet right onto my feet. It was a transparent and clumsy way to capture my attention. Colorful credit cards, coins in all sizes, dollar bills and small slips of paper rained onto my high-heeled shoes. Lightheartedly I laughed out loud, especially when he attempted to pick up the disarray graciously but the coins escaped his fingers. Cupid seized his opportunity. The third Cupid arrow of my life pierced the center of my heart, unnoticed, while I was laughing, feeling light and silly. Spicy small talk evolved. I stayed for another hour, chatting, flirting, happy. Cupid was content. I envision him strolling away, muttering to himself, "No more shots for her." Andy and I married in 1990.

Exhilaration was missing in my array of feelings. There were, however, a new optimism and a sense of well-being. We started our hopeful new household in Boca with three teenagers: Robert, my son; and Eric and Elizabeth, his two children. Theoretically all odds were in our favor. Andy and I both had struggled through and earned the difficult CPA certification. We also were both crazy about animals, especially dogs. We enjoyed traveling in Europe, and we loved to laugh and cook and run our busy household.

Gradually, a deep connection grew between us. I began to feel safe again and treasured our togetherness. I felt happy in a serene way. It was an absence of mental anguish, loneliness, disappointment and a presence of warmth, purpose and an ability to handle life's normal small annoyances. My seemingly stable home life lent me strength to take on new tasks.

In this spirit, after a few years I left the world of finance and studied Nursing at Broward Community College. This led to my RN certification in 1995. It also led Andy to wile away many lonely hours while I was either at school, at work or studying. Together we had saved enough money to purchase six townhouses in Boca Gardens. As a new landlady I took care of them lovingly, which occupied additional time. I became absorbed by my activities and was unaware of my husband's gradual change in demeanor toward me.

While gratitude for my interesting and love-filled life still grew innocently, bad forces had already started covertly to tear it all apart again. Andy was able to control his substance addiction only temporarily. In the fourth year of our marriage, he finally slipped. I had known that he savored his daily scotches. Yet, I had never seen him drunk. I also had never known about the Percocet with which he enhanced the alcohol's effect. Disaster struck our family without forewarning on a warm summer evening.

Andy arrived home late from work. I had planned a rare, cozy dinner for the two of us. When I saw him, I couldn't believe my eyes. He looked disheveled. His light-green shirt wasn't tucked into his belt and the fabric hung down to his hips. Thick, untamed strands of his normally well-groomed, dark hair fell over his forehead. I was alone with him; all three kids were busy with their own activities.

His eyes expressed rage. His pupils were fixated on me. What I saw swinging from his right hand took my breath, and I began to shiver. He was clutching a sledge hammer the size of a grapefruit. His body swayed drunkenly as he stepped toward me. Stunned and horrified, I backed away toward the dining room table. His speech was still clear, but he literally spit the words into my face one by one: "I'll... kill... you, you...#%@$!" Without effort, he started lifting the heavy hammer. My instincts took over. I plunged onto my knees and rapidly crawled away from him beneath the table. Above my head an explosion; the hammer crashed into the polished oak of the table. The impact shook the floor under my knees. Without looking back I scrambled to the door and ran out into the street. My heart was racing when I knocked on a neighbor's door.

This episode started my existence under recurring domestic abuse. It continued until 1997. Only then did I finally gather the courage to leave Andy for good. To appease him, I left him the townhouses, our residence and my car. It worked; I'm still alive and well. Statistics are clear: most victims of domestic violence are killed around the time when they seriously attempt to leave the relationship.

My third divorce was granted in 1997. Single, working mother for the third time, 49 years old. Robert was 24. He was supportive in every way. My son had grown into a responsible, decent young man. I changed my RN part-time position at the local hospital to full-time. My income was sufficient. My parents helped me with the purchase of a new residence and a car.

My 1997 divorce left me with an overriding feeling of great relief. Other identifiable perceptions at the time were a strong desire to re-establish peace of mind and stability. Another consequence of this breakup was my adopting Greta Garbo's somber attitude: "I *vant* to be alone!"

And so I stayed alone. Very, very alone. Cupid probably checked on me once in a while, but he must have always flown off, disappointed, recognizing that his efforts would be futile. In 2003, I returned to work in the financial sector. Until the end of 2008 I immersed myself in my work. All my affections were spent on my son, my parents, my animals. I locked away my spirit and my soul to never be hurt again by any man.

Toward the end of 2008, I retired. Within weeks I started to feel empty and without direction. The dark cloud of depression hovered right above me, ready to sweep down and engulf me. But my dogs kept me smiling and busy. I walked them twice a day.

Eventually I met several other dog-loving neighbors. One of them was Lilliane, a spirited, courageous, Russian-born woman with an abounding love life. We quickly became good friends. She had come to the U.S. as a mail-order bride. Her men-stories were endless and fascinating. Did she alert Cupid as to my availability or was it the other way around? We'll never know; but invariably, every time we met to go shopping or to the movies, there was a moment when she looked at me intensely and said, "You need MAN." Her intonation of these three words always had me laugh.

Usually I would quickly imitate her enunciation: "...and you need English lessons." As the friendship took its course, we chatted, laughed, cried and bantered over life's complexities.

But Lilliane stuck to her guns: "You need man."

One afternoon, she said, "Let's look computer." She meant to check out Internet dating sites. I'm tempted to believe that a little cyber-Cupid, paunchy from lack of exercise, sits inside the computer and meddles with the search results. "Men between 60 and 69." The first hits were only mildly interesting. I imagine him becoming frustrated. He might have pulled my file, checked the records, glanced at my birth date.

A frowning Cupid mumbled to himself, "Hmm. Should I even bother, at *her* age?" Meanwhile, work orders for his arrow service poured in by the hundreds. He felt pressured for time and had to make a quick decision. "OK! Why not?" His own love and happiness with Princess Psyche normally sets him into a generous mood. He swiftly re-arranged the order of my search results so that a sweet-looking guy appeared on top of page one.

"That's better," I said to Lilliane.

Relieved Cupid reaches for his arrow and aims with the intensity of a sniper…ah, full hit into the sweet spot!

Now please re-read the first few paragraphs of this story…

On ne choisit pas qui on est mais qui on devient

One Does Not Choose Who One Is but Who One Becomes

Marion Hottier

Marion Hottier was a guest of ours this summer. From the village of Villerupt in the Lorraine area of France bordering Belgium, Germany, and Luxembourg, she arrived in the U.S. for the first time with her grandparents and her cousin Loup ("Wolf") to visit my former French teacher and friend, Melissa. At thirteen, Marion has the legs of a filly (the French word for girl is "fille"), the exuberance of youth, and the intensity of a budding woman. We all found her delightful. As we talked together, I learned that she longed to see beyond the farm where she grew up, so coming to America was a great thrill. Marion has dreams of becoming an interior designer. She took photos of all the food she ate and wrote in her journal every day. When she returned home, I asked her to write about her life and impressions from her trip. In Marion you will find wisdom beyond her years.

My name is Marion; I am thirteen-and-a-half years old. I live in Lorraine. I grew up in a small village of 450 people with my mother, who works for an American organization, my father, a stockbreeding farmer, and my brother who is fifteen-and-a-half, a student in a school of professional agriculture; and not to forget the dog Domino and the cat Minette!

I lived my first twelve years on an old renovated farm, where our parents had settled into a quiet life. My brother and I spent the greater part of each day at the home of the babysitter, Tata Lili, because our parents worked and because of our young age. She lived in another village.

When we were old enough to enter the school, we were still under the care of Tata Lili. We went to the school in her village and had lunch at her house each noon. She would come for us after school and we would stay with her until my mother returned to claim us. Tata Lili would help us with our homework and permit us to watch a little television.

At that time, my extracurricular activities like dance and music were very important to me. They allowed me to be proud of myself, and proved to me the (French) adage that says, *Quand on veut on peut.* "When one wants, one can."

Weekends and days off followed the rhythms of my father's work, with outings in the forest or on the farm, where the chickens, the cows, and the pigs amused me as much as my brother's antics. For vacations we rarely left, but in winter *Maman* would take us skiing in the Alps. Summer was always devoted to work in the fields to ensure a good harvest. Though we could never leave long enough for a complete vacation, I was happy that my mom and I could take some days to escape and make some nice discoveries in France. In this way, we have been able to visit some beautiful regions of France, including Poitou, Normandy, and Vendée. I remember also spending a good number of vacation days with my maternal grandparents, busy doing housework with my grandmother or afternoon shopping (which I love!!).

As I grow older, the activities and family centers of interest, particularly those of my father, do not truly amuse or interest me. My father does not understand this, which makes our father-daughter relationship rather difficult and it is still difficult today.

One day I understood that all that was would not be anymore; my parents divorced. Personally I took it rather well; isn't it truly more agreeable to have parents happy but separate, rather than obligated to live together and to see them ignore each other all day long in a house where the atmosphere is so heavy that you get bored with it?

My brother and I had the good fortune to have intelligent parents who permitted us the choice of with whom we would live. Very logically according to our characters, my brother chose to stay at the farm with our father and I chose to follow my mother.

The farm where the four of us lived belongs to my father's family; *Maman* and I went to live in a neighboring village about eight miles away. As a matter of fact, it's the same village where I am going to high school, so I will not have to change schools. And so for the last year we girls have lived in an apartment smaller than the house and in a small town of 10,000 inhabitants, considerably larger than the village where I grew up!

I can also choose when I wish to see my father. I adapt my visits to his house when I have time and when his schedule allows, but when my father is not available I make the best of these moments by going out with childhood friends, having fun, and forgetting about school!

Next September I pass into third level, which in France is similar to your 9th grade. Then three years at *Lycée* toward completing my secondary education and earning my diploma (in France this is called the *baccalaureate*). It is an important year because I wish to have a choice in work that pleases me, and for that it is necessary to study and acquire my degrees. I would like very much to be an interior designer or work in a creative medium like photography. So that will mean time at university too!

In imagining my future, I see myself in the United States, living in a beautiful house; I have created a studio of photographic design that has made me a little famous...but this is not only my imagination. I am aware that imagination is the start of dreams, but I must take the necessary actions to make them real. And sometimes a dream-come-true just happens to you, perhaps because wishing makes it so. I thought I would never be in the United States, and only today I returned after twenty days there and would love to go back again! It was the most incredible voyage of my life, a dream awakened that became a reality.

On the 18th of June 2010 we departed from Paris, destination Washington, D.C. to visit Melissa. My grandparents served as her host family when she studied in France, so my mother shared her home with Melissa when they were both sixteen. My mother always kept in touch with her as the years passed. At Melissa's urging, my grandparents finally decided to make the trip and spend some time at her home in Alexandria, Virginia. After much discussion and some last-minute planning, it was also decided that I would accompany them, along with my cousin Loup. It was for me an occasion I could not begin to realize in my dreams, to see the country that would one day be so welcoming to me!

It is in this way that we visited the Appalachians, North and South Carolina, Florida, Washington, D.C. and the surrounding area. I found the country very different from France as far as culture, the size and the landscape. The journey was very pleasant. We stayed at the homes of people truly wonderful and welcoming, and there I discovered areas diversified and magnificent.

What could be more fantastic than lying in the sun on the beach in Vero Beach, a visit to the Everglades and the alligators, the Blue Ridge lining the horizon at Grandfather Mountain, the historic houses of Charleston, or the annual 4th of July celebration and the fireworks in Washington, D.C.! And the height of fun for a girl of my age: the gigantic commercial center (Mall!) with all the madness and extravagances in a spectacular unfolding of colors, scents and flavors.

I hold wonderful memories because I realized part of my dream, and because I met people I can never thank enough; a part of my heart remains there.

Now I know that I will return one day, whether to live in the U.S. or spend a few days, only the future can say. But I will return there — that is certain!

Prairie Skies to PowerPoint

Marlowe Olson Arnold

Marlowe Olson Arnold is a talented writer of children's stories who has also published a book of her poems and paintings called **On Butterfly Wings.** *Born in North Dakota, Marlowe found her way to Vero Beach, Florida in 1971. She worked as a children's librarian and as a children's book reviewer for Scripps Treasure Coast Newspapers. Supposedly "retired," she is currently an adjunct instructor in English at Indian River State College. Marlowe is also a gardener, a good listener and a delightful person to know; but her proudest accomplishment is making a difference in the education, and thus the lives, of young people.*

As a woman in the 21st century, my life has spanned a technological age that is still exploding—the advent of the computer, the reality of walking on the moon, the discovery of nuclear power, the trend of reading newspapers electronically. The limitlessness of further knowledge is more vast than the Dakota prairie skies under which I was born.

Through my teaching years, learning and teaching have been interwoven. I have learned, with my students, to see possibilities, to recognize differences, to be curious, to value facts. The story is that when Archimedes discovered the principle of specific gravity he leaped out of his bathtub shouting, "Eureka!" — "I have found it!" There is excitement in learning.

My teaching experiences have also been learning experiences. One of my first English teaching positions was at a high school in Delray Beach, Florida. I had six classes of freshman English. It was a challenge. The honors class was simmering along with Shakespeare and poetry, but the regular classes were struggling, particularly one class. I soon realized that many of these students hated to write; of course, in English classes, writing essays is necessary. Not only did they hate writing, but they also seemed afraid; they seemed to freeze when a writing assignment was given. I told them the story about Churchill who had said that he was once afraid of a blank canvas until he decided to paint in big, bold strokes. I told the students to think of their papers as blank canvases and write without fear as Churchill painted. "Don't let the blank paper intimidate you. Just put words down," I admonished. Some of the students smiled and the idea seemed to help, but others were still frustrated.

I decided to try another approach. Since Seacrest High School was located near the Atlantic Ocean, I decided to use words like *beach, seaweed, sand, surfing.* I wrote one word on the board at a time and let them write for five minutes on each word. The idea worked. They were writing and not just sitting in a daze or crumpling papers to throw in the basket. One fellow came to me after class and said, "Mrs. Arnold, I may not be your best student in English class, but on the beach I'm the best surfer, and this paper was fun to write." From this point on, I realized more imaginative teaching was necessary; sometimes students needed to be engaged before they would be connected to the learning process.

Once I took a position as a reading teacher for Title I — pull-out classes for students on free or reduced-cost lunch programs. Here I realized more about teaching/learning. These children had failed to pass their grade, so they were being retained for further instruction. I was aware that children learned according to different modalities. I would hold a card with a word, tell them to look at it, then cover the word and ask them to tell me the word they just saw. We also had fun printing words in the air. We would listen and sing words. I would tell them to close their eyes and ask them if they could see the word in print. We even printed words in the sand outside the portable classroom. Every child was valuable. When the year was over, the parents were invited to an afternoon of reading. We had not planned for refreshments. There was no budget. But I will never forget how one student brought a large bag of chips and another student bought a big soda bottle to share for our reading party. These students did not have much materially, but they were proud of their accomplishments and they wanted to celebrate. Hopefully, their success in learning to read will become a lifetime of reading.

I have always wanted to present reading as a joyous explorative adventure where the excitement of the story would give the joy of reading. For example, in Jack London's great read-aloud story, "To Build a Fire," it is not necessary for every student to analyze the story as it fits in the school of naturalism. I believe it is enough to read it as a great adventure and to realize that the dog's instinct was truer than the man's foolish judgment. In Shirley Jackson's shocking short story, "Lottery," if the reader understands that just because something has always been done does not make it morally or ethically right, the student has learned a principle of living. Reading has opened a door to learning and given clarity to our jumbled lives.

For several years I was an elementary school librarian. One of the major events during the years was Character Day — the students dressed like the characters from the books they were reading. I remember one fellow dressing like Charles Lindbergh and strapping molded airplane wings around his waist. When Christmas came we studied Christmas customs from various countries. On St. Lucia Day (a special Swedish holiday), the student library aides dressed as St. Lucia and Star Boys, and went to every classroom bringing *lussekats* (buns) and coffee to the teachers. One of the parents built a small puppet theater and the students acted out stories like Lobel's "Frog and Toad" and Marshall's "George and Martha." The stories became alive.

Today, in my college classes, we are writing poems to paintings and using PowerPoint graphics to show the connections of images to words. Teaching is an intellectual awakening. Learning is a becoming: a living with never enough years to discover all one desires to learn.

Changing Descartes' famous quote, I would say, "I teach, therefore I am."

The Queen of Heartless

Marsha Foresman

Marsha Foresman earned a masters degree in Labor & Industrial Relations and made her career with the Michigan Department of Corrections. She is writing a book about her experiences. Never one to rest on her laurels, she enjoys an active and well-deserved retirement, dividing her time between Tucson and Traverse City. Marsha was the person who told me that the engagement ring is worn on top of the wedding band, because (depending on how you look at it) the diamond is worn closest to the heart. Now, here she is, the Queen of Heartless.

I am the Queen of Heartless, or I was for five years. I chopped off the heads of prison guards, probation officers, maintenance employees and nurses. I sent them packing for five-, ten-, or thirty-day suspensions; discharged and demoted them. In five years, I managed to fire over 500 employees and issue suspension without pay for over 6,000 employees of the Michigan Department of Corrections. I declared, "Off with their heads!" on a daily basis.

They deserved it! They exhibited dangerous behavior and some of them should have been on the other side of the bars. On the other hand, some of them were just plain dumb.

Take the case of the prison guard from a maximum security facility in the Upper Peninsula of Michigan who by day guarded murderers, rapists and drug dealers and by night ran his own marijuana farm. Since the growing season in the Upper Peninsula of Michigan is roughly ten weeks long, this genius planted his marijuana plants in a spare room off his garage. Even if you don't believe the growing of marijuana should be a crime, the fact of the matter is that such behavior constitutes a crime in Michigan and prison guards are sworn to uphold the laws of the State. In the winter of 1999, Officer M's crop was proving to be a banner year. The plants were over five feet high and healthy. Officer M was so proud of his achievement he took pictures of his crop and sent the roll of film into the local One-Hour Photography store. Not only did he put his name and telephone number on the return envelope, but his pictures included his truck with the license clearly showing. After developing the pictures, the owner of the photography store called the Drug Enforcement Administration, reported the crime, and the DEA raided the officer's home and took him off to the local jail, charging him with a felony.

The next morning, the sheriff called the warden of the prison to tell him that he had locked up an officer who was supposed to have reported for duty at 6 a.m. The warden called me to determine whether he could have permission to fire the man on the spot. Obviously, felonious behavior warranted discharge, but the warden felt that the worse crime was stupidity and could hardly keep from laughing.

Discipline of public employees in a state which is heavily unionized, such as Michigan, conforms to rules which are spelled out in collective bargaining agreements (union contracts). Employees must be given notice and a hearing before they can be disciplined or discharged. Over the years, the strength of the unions has not only centered on their ability to gain higher wages, but more importantly to defend employees against management's disciplinary actions. Employees expect unions to save their jobs even in the face of the employee's rule violations or his own stupidity. But this isn't a treatise on labor relations or management rights. This is a story of human foibles that affect the effective running of prisons, parole offices and probation offices. This is a story of impediments to keeping the public safe. In short, these stories are your tax dollars hard at work.

ABUSE OF FORCE

Our nation has been undergoing a dialogue regarding treatment of prisoners, whether they are accused terrorists, convicted felons or detained illegal aliens. It has been a long-determined position of correctional experts that abusing prisoners is anathema to running safe and secure prisons. For this reason, Employee Rules in Michigan declared that abuse of a prisoner would subject an employee to discipline up to and including discharge. But what constitutes abuse? Obviously, beating or raping a prisoner constitutes abuse. But what about psychological torment, or sexual groping under the guise of conducting a legitimate pat-down search? Too often, the code of silence among officers hid dirty secrets. Too often, the fear of retribution from officers made female prisoners submit to humiliation.

During my five year "reign" I tried to chop down abuse whenever investigators brought evidence to support the claim. In some cases, the Department was successful in discharging abusers; in others we had to reinstate those officers after an arbitrator ordered such reinstatement.

THE CASE OF THE BEATING IN THE SHOWER

A segregation unit in a prison is usually referred to as a "jail within a jail." Prisoners are confined to segregation after they have violated prison rules or have been determined to be a threat to themselves or others, both prisoners and staff. Segregated prisoners are confined to their cells twenty-three out of twenty-four hours a day, may be denied the use of their property, may be denied access to recreation, and are always moved out of their cells by two officers. They are, however, entitled to adequate health care, food, access to legal materials and hygiene access such as showers and, of course, to be free from abuse.

Segregated prisoners are often loud, abusive and generally "mouthy." If they get abusive to staff, they can be assessed a disciplinary sanction which can result in an assessment of more time in segregation or loss of items such as noted above. Staff are never permitted to seek physical revenge on prisoners who aggravate them. The Michigan rules specifically tell staff that any abuse of prisoners will result in discharge.

Prisoner K was a mouthy prisoner. He yelled at staff and seemed to have a penchant for yelling at Officer Rabs. Officer Rabs had little patience with the prisoner and even told the night shift sergeant that this prisoner was "a pain in the ass" and the sergeant needed to "straighten him out." Prisoner K was diabetic and needed an insulin shot every day, which was administered by a nurse.

One weekend afternoon Prisoner K was especially loud and demanding as the afternoon shift came on duty. As such at the beginning of the shift, Officer Rabs determined that he would be denied a shower. To cover this refusal, Officer Rabs wrote a psychiatric referral claiming that the prisoner was yelling and claiming to hear voices and therefore should not be allowed out of his cell.

Later, towards the end of the shift, Officer Rabs and his partner, Officer Clu, went to the prisoner's cell and informed him that they were now going to allow him to take a shower. The prisoner undressed, was handcuffed behind his back and taken from his cell to the shower area. At that point, Officer Rabs threw him violently against the wall, put a choke hold on his throat and began hitting him in the torso with fists; all while saying, "I'm tired of your shit!"

The assault continued until Officer Clu stopped Officer Rabs by saying, "He's had enough." The prisoner was returned to his cell, and although the shower area was not in full view of the unit, two other prisoners witnessed the entire assault.

After Officer Rabs left for the evening, Prisoner K attempted to talk to the night shift sergeant to obtain medical treatment. There was no health care staff available, but the night shift sergeant talked to Prisoner K, noted that he was hurting and that the usually loud prisoner had trouble talking.

On Sunday, when the nurse stopped by his cell to administer Prisoner K's insulin, Officer Rabs came with her and the prisoner was unable to talk confidentially with the nurse. He tried to slip a note to another officer on another shift, but the officer thought he was lying and ripped up the note. Finally, during the week, when counseling staff came back to work, Prisoner K informed his prison counselor of the assault. The counselor reported the incident to Internal Affairs and the investigation was on.

Officers Rabs and Clu were immediately transferred out of the unit and the investigator talked to all of the prisoners in the unit and found the two who had witnessed the assault. During the investigation, Officer Rabs called the unit and asked to talk to one of the prisoner witnesses. Although such action is strictly prohibited, a junior officer permitted Officer Rabs to talk with the witness. Rabs pressured the prisoner into refraining from testifying by threatening him with future retribution. This witness eventually informed the investigator of the threats and his testimony was used against Officer Rabs.

Generally speaking, arbitrators do not give equal credence to prisoner statements over those of staff. However, after a long hearing, the arbitrator felt the threatening behavior of Officer Rabs to be distressing. His concern that the officer found it necessary to pressure the prisoner-witness led him to find Prisoner K and the other prisoner witnesses to be truthful.

It was always important to me to enforce employee rules, to represent management fairly, to hear all sides, and to keep the public interest—and the tax dollars spent at their expense—in mind. In this case, the arbitrator upheld the discharges; the "heads stayed off!"

On Engineering Climate Control Systems

or

Is it Hot in Here? Is it Cold in Here?

Martha Nefcy

Martha Nefcy is an incredible combination of statuesque beauty, intelligence, sportsmanship and professional competence. She is genuinely funny, a quality that has served her in dealing with obstacles to her career aspirations as a design engineer (specializing in car heating and cooling systems) in the male-dominated automotive industry. When I first met her I was in high school, and she was my girlfriend's five-year-old sister. The next time I saw Martha was forty years later, at pre-wedding festivities for a couple of mutual acquaintance. She was seated at a table in a little bistro, captivating the crowd with scandalous stories and slightly sarcastic remarks. Suddenly I realized who she was and asked, "Little Martha, is that you?" It was indeed.

With over twenty-five years in the automotive industry, I have seen many changes. My stories are about how women were treated in a traditional man's profession, and how I had to adapt to survive and thrive. The stories describe how I was shaped into a confident and capable engineer, mostly in spite of the treatment of women in the auto industry.

During my career I always had to earn my stripes. Being a woman in a male-dominated field, you are always a target. *What is she wearing? How is she styling her hair? Why is she so emotional? What do you suppose she does when she's not at work?* Maybe they just don't have any fun in their lives and need to use me to get it, not sure. However, each team you work with must learn how you operate and what your agenda is. Over time I have delivered on countless commitments and have earned a reputation for dealing fairly and logically from a strong technical base. I delivered function, cost, and quality on many projects to earn that reputation. Continuing to have to prove myself more so than my male peers is my lot.

As a young engineering trainee, I tested returned parts from engine control circuit boards. I then wrote a report and typed a letter to the supplier requesting they address the component quality issues I had discovered. I had a male senior engineer directing me in this matter. He, too, had done some diagnostics, and wanted me to type his letter to his supplier. Of course I was reluctant but wanted to set a precedent with my response. Computers had been recently put on all engineers' desks, and I offered to teach him how to use the word processing program. But I refused to do his typing for him. He was quite upset with me.

"Why not?" he asked. I simply stated that I had been hired as an engineer, not a secretary. "We are going to have to take this to our supervisor," he added.

"OK, let's go!"

I had no idea what the supervisor would say. He listened to the senior engineer whine, "Martha won't do my typing for me."

The supervisor asked me if this were true, and I said it was but that I had not been hired to do typing. I had been hired to do engineering and that I had offered to train him in the tools. Needless to say, I was happy when the supervisor directed the senior engineer to learn how to use the tools and do his own typing, reinforcing the fact that I was not employed as a secretary. Whew! I dodged a bullet on that one!

Once during a supplier visit, I was reviewing the plant operation and the quality process documents and asking many questions about their statistical process control capability. When the tour was over and we were back in a conference room, I stated my observations and conclusions, and asked technical questions looking for answers. The plant manager was quite confused with all my questions. Why had his guys not brought the OEM engineer with them for this review?

The room was very silent as everyone except the plant manger knew *I* was the OEM engineer on these products. They waited for me to say something. I indicated that I was the engineer responsible for the design and was not questioning the design, but rather the process capability at this plant, since I had observed several areas of concern.

The plant manager had one foot in his mouth and seemed determined to get the other one in there too. He claimed that there were so many "gals" from Purchasing he just thought I was one of them, basically insulting me and my technical background. Apparently he had not encountered female engineers before. I politely corrected him, and his face flushed with discomfort at the gaffe he had made.

This awkward situation passed and I thought I would not ever hear from that plant manager again. A few days went by, and then a dozen long-stemmed yellow roses arrived at my desk with a sincere apology on the card. I later learned that the embarrassed plant manager had told his wife and daughter about his major blunder and what an idiot he had made of himself. They were horrified and directed him to make amends. Thus, the roses. I think many men changed their views about women in the workforce when they got hit up for their double standards at the dinner table by their own wives and daughters. The roses served as a reminder, I think, to accept female engineers on their merit.

I often like to use my smile and humor to diffuse a tense situation. One of my coworkers, Gene, seemed to enjoy getting a reaction from me, probably since I was the only woman in the department except for the administrative assistant. He said outlandish things, told dirty jokes, made suggestive comments — all to get me to react somehow (cry, blush, fly off the handle). I was used to components with very small-gauge wire 22 that you could rip the insulation off of with your fingernails. One day I was building a bench model of my components; and, in trying not to break the copper strands, he saw me struggling with larger 14-gauge wires and trying to gently strip the insulation from them. *Gentleman Gene* grabbed the wire strippers from me and did it himself. He was stronger and stripped the wires in no time.

A day later he overheard my part of a conversation with a supplier about component connectors and who owned which connector half. When a group of supplier reps came to take Gene to lunch he introduced me to them as being the "new, very green, wet behind the ears" engineer to whom he had to teach the ropes. He teased me in front of these new people, saying that he had to teach me how to "strip," as well as the difference between male and female. He didn't say strip *wire* or male/female *connectors*.

I had taken about enough from this guy, and decided to let him have it. I smiled at him and the other group members and gently started unbuttoning my suit jacket, pulled at my floppy bow, and untied it very slowly. "Yes," I told the crowd that had now gathered, "Gene taught me everything I know and now I'm learning to strip really well." I then began to remove my jacket suggestively. At this point Gene was turning numerous shades of red and was starting to leap over the desk partition to run away. Funny, he never bothered me again!

On another occasion I was invited to a supplier golf outing with many people from my department. It was assumed that I did not golf because I was female and therefore only invited for lunch. Just as I was being introduced to the head of the company, these two large bouncer types showed up on either side of me and asked me to leave. This caught me by surprise, and I had to ask why. It was because I was a woman in a room designated for MEN ONLY. I was shocked! I wasn't invited because I was male or female; I was invited because I was the OEM lead engineer on the components that this supplier manufactured. I was humiliated, but I didn't want to make it easy by bowing out, so I stated that I thought the entire party should move to another, more appropriate room. I mean, if you are going to have a golf outing with a customer, at least assume there *might* be some women along and do not schedule an exclusive room. The supplier was Japanese, and I think women must have been further behind in their workforce, as they thought their behavior was normal.

They couldn't move the entire party because no other room was available to accommodate such a large group. Instead, they just moved a small table of us to another room for lunch. The outcast table.

After lunch, the president of the company came over and spoke in Japanese to my sales representative. "Will this affect our relationship?" was translated for my benefit.

"Absolutely," was my response. Some words were spoken in Japanese that didn't sound pleasant. Then the president turned to me and, speaking in English, apologized and asked if I was staying for golf. I answered that I had not been invited for golf. More stern-sounding words were exchanged in Japanese. He smiled and asked if I actually was a golfer. I responded that I absolutely was. More rapid-fire words were directed to the man on my left. The president then offered to have me outfitted in the clubhouse with all the clothes, shoes, clubs, and golf equipment I would need in order to play—at his expense. Our company policy does not allow us to accept such gifts so, naturally, I had to decline.

A couple of weeks later I received a call from that same supplier inviting me to the same country club for a similar golf outing. *Except*, they were looking for my husband, because some conscientious employee had placed a star next to my name and the caller assumed I was male. I declined to go through that experience again. Golf as a business tool was becoming less and less appealing in this situation—I imagine for both parties.

When I became a new manager in an area in which I did not consider myself an expert, I found the supervisors working for me throwing me under the bus at every opportunity. I found it funny that they enjoyed putting me on the spot to see how I would react. I called it the E.F. Hutton syndrome. Everyone would turn, the room would fall silent, and all would bend an ear toward me to see what I would say. Of course, I always responded to the questions with the most intelligent comment I could muster. The look on their faces was always the same —"Wow, she has a brain!" I earned my stripes again and again.

Along my way in the engineering world, I decided that I did not just want to *work*; I wanted a career in which I could really enjoy what I was doing. I mean, if you have to work, you might as well like it. So I chose to be happy about coming to work each day, and to give my very best at all times. I think I am a better performer because of my choices. I am a high-energy person who gets a lot done. I believe being happy every day is a choice —even for a woman in the automotive industry.

These events and more have shaped who I am. I don't put up with guff from anyone. I have always been confident, and I figured out quickly that I could be an expert in anything where I decided to be an expert. I have learned that many men are lacking in self-assurance, even though they may outwardly appear to ooze confidence. This is not necessarily a male thing; sounding confident is part of success. Doing is the rest. I have learned to be at ease with sounding good even when I ad lib the next steps. I have learned that I am very valuable to coworkers as a team member and leader. Everyone can appreciate that under my tutelage we will be a winning team—and we'll have fun along the way.

Mary Ellen the Clown

Mary Ellen Clark

My first encounters with Mary Ellen Clark were as a friend of my mother's in the neighborhood where I grew up. She was always coming up with tickets to a show at the Fox Theatre (all you had to do was usher for the show), or letting us know about singing, dance, and musical performances featuring her children. Before anyone heard of Harry Potter, the Clarks were amazing kids on the block with their magic tricks. Then I learned they were also talented actors and several starred in local plays. The clown career was the last thing I learned about, when Mary Ellen agreed to put on a show for my sister's second grade class. Her story is a wonderful one, about all the people in show business you never hear of, but have no less talent or derive any less enjoyment from their work. To entertain is to offer a great gift to the world. Fame is, perhaps, just another illusion.

When I married forty-nine years ago, I was a classical singer specializing in coloratura, and a full-time vocational home economics teacher of foods classes in a Detroit high school. When I started having children, I did substitute teaching and learned how to deal with elementary school children. At one point I filled in for kindergarten teachers who didn't leave me lesson plans. They liked my plans and said I would make a good pre-school teacher.

When my oldest was in kindergarten and the ones who followed were three-and-a-half and two years old, I started teaching the children of my friends two mornings a week in reading, music, science, math, writing, and art. I had taken courses in the Montessori Method. You are to introduce the children to many different experiences, observe and build on their strengths. My own children were talented in the arts, so I helped them learn to sing in harmony, to do puppetry, took them to tap dancing lessons, taught them magic tricks, how to play the piano and how to juggle. They excelled in all these areas.

When they reached the ages of seven, nine and eleven, respectively, I thought we had enough acts to do a thirty-minute show. My husband's boss at the Schools Center Building in Detroit, the administrative area of the Detroit Public Schools, was giving his daughter a birthday party. We five (my husband and I, our two sons and our daughter) volunteered to entertain. Someone at that party saw us and invited us to perform for a Cub Scout banquet. My older son was shy, but would perform if we let him dress up as a clown. His younger brother wanted to do the same. We used the clothes from our dress-up corner and used water soluble clown white for their faces. Then my daughter and my husband wanted to do get into the act. I made simple matching costumes eventually for all of us, got wigs for the children and a hobo hat for my husband. I didn't wear makeup because it took too long to help the others with theirs. It wasn't until my oldest son was thirteen and started to get acne that I took his clown face. He no longer wore clown makeup and had gotten over his shyness.

That is how I came to be a clown.

As time went on, one show led to another and organizations we joined helped us to become known. We joined the Detroit Puppeteers Guild and Puppeteers of America, performed magic with the Tel-Twelve Mystics, and played with The Society for the Preservation and the Advancement of the Harmonica when we added chord, bass and chromatic harmonicas to the show. I learned to play the Chord. We joined the World Clown Association. People from these organizations recommended us to booking agencies.

We kept honing our skills and practicing. I was in charge of taking the children to lessons such as tap dancing, copying the routines on paper so I could tell them what came next as they practiced. I taught them how to play the piano. They took guitar lessons together so they could sing and play together. I taught them how to sing in harmony. One son learned to play the double bass, for which there were lessons and orchestra rehearsals, summer camps, and other venues.

I got them started in juggling and then we found a teacher and a juggling club. There were club meetings in the various organizations and conventions, which led to more learning. Each new talent and skill was added to enhance the shows.

My husband was in charge of booking, bookkeeping, public relations, driving, hauling, and purchasing the many things such as musical instruments, sound systems, props, lighting, and so on. He was the artistic director, coming up with new ideas and new material he thought would make the show more appealing. During the week he had a regular 9 to 5 job with the Detroit Public Schools. At one point, he took all of our TVs and put them on the curb. For five years we had no TV and lots of time to practice after dinner without distractions.

After school time I supervised the tap-dancing practice, and when friends came over they got to watch the practice before they went out to play. The boys came up with a comedy routine as they lay in their bunk beds imitating cartoon characters and movie stars. We would start the show with circus music and clown skits, then a puppet show with the children as the puppeteers and my husband and I in front of the puppet theater playing harmonicas. A tap dance routine would follow with all three children. I had to remember to put resin on the floor! Each of us would do a magic trick, one son did the juggling, we would sing about three numbers in harmony, and then play some harmonica selections. As the children learned to play guitars, bass fiddle and keyboard, they were added to the repertoire. Sometimes we hired a drummer. It became an hour show. I sewed backdrop curtains, liners for the carts we used to carry equipment, many covers and bags for transport and storage, curtains for the puppet theater, and renewed costumes through the years.

We expanded our performance and entertainment into doing outdoor games for company picnics, indoor games for other occasions, as well as learning to twist balloons into animals and other shapes, and we learned to do face painting. This made us more well-rounded and versatile.

When we started to advertise, we were noticed by a number

of local agencies as well as other groups, and spent many weekends doing shows in schools, birthday parties, company parties, fairs and festivals. Living in a major city and entertaining for over thirty years took us many places we would not have experienced otherwise. We have met many celebrities and have performed for them or have been on the same bill with them.

In order to do this I had to make sure that everything was ready for packing: props, equipment, instruments, tricks, puppets, tap shoes, juggling equipment, etc. I prayed as we traveled that I didn't forget anything, and sometimes I did, even with a check list. Before we would leave, I had to prepare a meal or pack one if we were not eating at a banquet. There was the makeup to apply and costumes to prepare. Multiple things to do and plan. We needed lots of time to get ready.

Many of our friends became our audiences as we practiced our routines in their homes. Grandma and Grandpa watched us in their living room more than any others, and at one point Grandpa built the first puppet theater. They both bought us many puppets. Our audiences have varied, from families to the elderly to the handicapped. Our shows are non-violent, wholesome fun.

As the children became young adults, they left the family show one by one. We had to adjust the show to fit those who remained. Today, each one has their own entertainment business and I do my own shows. I do many of the same tasks, except that I am the sole performer. In trying to continue to be versatile, I have developed many themed shows, some for the holidays, as well as on specific topics. I have a Train Show, Fish Show,

Dinosaur Show, Around the World Show, Fairy Tale Show (as Mother Goose), Bunny Show, and a Science Show. When he can, my husband packs and unpacks the car, drives me to a location and sometimes stays if I need him as a stagehand. I accept challenges such as being a music teacher for a preschool, planning and teaching a week-long drama course at a summer camp, being an MC at functions, and continuing to do face painting, balloons and games.

Now I have the challenge of the computer and how to use it to improve my business. I try to stay in shape by exercising on a bike and weightlifting. This job requires a lot of stamina. After thirty-five years I have collected many props to go with the different themes, and the time has come to downsize. There are many facets to show business that no one ever sees—lots of behind-the-scenes work. I feel as if I have been doing it all my life, because I started singing on stage and in the choir when I was about eight years old. Never did I think I would be doing it with my family. We ask ourselves, how did we get into this, why is it lasting so long, and was it meant to be? I guess it just felt right.

The Purple Teapot
Melissa S. Kerley, Ph.D.

Melissa Kerley was my first French teacher, chosen to help me learn a few phrases for travel. She taught private and group lessons in her home, taught foreign language at a private prep school, and started a business called **Speak Abroad**. *She had lived in France, been married to a Frenchman, and had a little white dog named Brigitte. Childlike and exuberant, she became quite dear to me. Eventually she moved to the Washington D.C. area, where she continues her work in education and teaches at a Montessori school. Imagine my surprise when she wrote about challenges representing an entirely different aspect of her life!*

I was six when the seizures came. The doctors ruled out epilepsy, but never did find out what brought them on. What the seizures caused, however, was clear. They weakened the right side of my body to such a degree that I couldn't walk normally, couldn't write legibly. My math and spatial relations abilities were essentially wiped out. My teachers told my parents I would probably never graduate high school. My doctors said I would never learn to ride a bike or swim.

My parents enrolled me in a special school through the third grade. Through the eighth grade I had special tutoring. I traced and reproduced so many series of three-dimensional and interlocking shapes in those classes that even now when I see the Olympic symbol those classes are all I can think about. Gym class was hell. Actually I played sick so often to miss gym class I almost couldn't graduate high school; my mother had to get my pediatrician to write a note to get me excused from all those missed classes. I did learn to swim though, and learned to ride a bike in a day (albeit a long day during which I received a great number of scratches and bruises). I finished high school, too. Later, I also earned a Ph.D.

I am incredibly fortunate to have had the parents that I did. I don't know how I would have managed to overcome the obstacles the seizures presented me with if they hadn't been there for me. It was my father who taught me to ride a bike. I was never told that I was not supposed to be able to learn. So when he offered me a pink-and-white frosted bike I was ready to go. He kept me out all day, refused outright to let me go inside until I could ride the bike. He was determined that I would not be disadvantaged in life. He is also the reason I made it through Algebra II in high school. Algebra II may not sound impressive; most people I know got through at least Pre-Calculus. But for me getting through Algebra II was huge.

My mother was a deeply caring and compassionate woman. She was also intensely creative. She played with me endlessly as a child, pushed me to imagine and create. She put up with the months when I wholeheartedly believed I was Cinderella, drove me all the way back through my bus route when I insisted that I had seen the most beautiful thing ever and that she absolutely had to see it too (only to excitedly point out a black-and-white spotted pig three-fourths of the way back to school). She edited and typed all my papers through my senior year of high school.

Most people I speak with don't know that the man who invented the self-check-in kiosks at airports has Attention Deficit Disorder (ADD); he invented the kiosks because he hated waiting in line. I learned this at a conference I attended several years back on the subject of learning differences. The speaker called learning differences "a gift that is difficult to unwrap." I would say that description is spot-on.

I am a teacher. When people cite my best quality as a teacher they always pick one of two: some people say it is my creativity; others say it is my devotion to my students. Both come from living with the learning differences the seizures left me. It is easy to think outside the box when you can't even see the box. And dealing with personal adversity certainly breeds compassion; at least it has for me.

My family moved quite often while I was growing up, so I had tutors in several different schools. In the fourth grade I was lumped in with all the other "special needs" students. What that meant was that my tutor was also the teacher for the mentally retarded kids. I found this fact humiliating; I didn't want my classmates to make fun of me. In order to convince me to come to my sessions, my tutor struck a deal with me: he would wait for me in the hall outside my classroom, and I would meet him there at the pre-determined time for our meeting. I have plenty of stories like that.

When I was growing up, my parents made sure I always understood I was successful in many ways and that they loved me. Still, it took a long time for me to accept that there were things I couldn't do as well as others, and that I would never be able to change my abilities with regard to those things. It took longer for me to decide that was all right, and to realize that some of the things I was good at had been fostered in compensation for — or as a distraction from — the things I wasn't good at. It has only been very recently that I have realized this is true for everyone, learning differences or not. I realized that we each have unique interests and talents that reflect who we are, that make even the most ordinary things special.

Years ago I had a dream. In it, a mentor of mine asked me to make him a teapot. I'm not sure what the point of that exercise was meant to be, but in the dream my mentor had a reason for asking me to make the teapot. I wanted to do as he had asked, but felt I had to give the teapot a certain flair, have it reflect who I was. So I painted it deep purple. Before the dream I had never seen a purple teapot. I have no idea how making my teapot that color became the signature I chose for it, although purple is a color I love, my color of choice through my artsy, funky twenties.

It wasn't until the day after my dream that I encountered a purple teapot. Still mulling over the dream, I had walked into a tea shop I frequented in town and asked if they had a purple teapot. They did, just one, the only one they had ever had or seen. It had come in very recently. I bought it. It is one of my most treasured possessions. I love it because it is original, because it is a discovery that came from somewhere deep within me. In my dream my mentor had looked at the teapot, cocked his head and scrunched together his eyebrows. He had said, "It's purple."

"Yeah" I said, "It's purple."

Gateways

Merana Cadorette

Merana Cadorette struck me as a flower-child when I first saw her, with her long wavy red hair and wearing a long linen dress. We were both authors with booths at a local book fair, and I was perusing the wares before the day commenced. We are both from big families and thus had an immediate connection. Merana has not followed a conventional career path, though she has worked as an educator and still works as a volunteer with the Girl Scouts. She has rebuilt and redecorated an airport hangar in Florida as an avant-garde second home, but has also painted classic watercolor gateways in the historic region of Savannah. Merana is a picture of opposites that come together as one fascinating person.

I have been lucky, and blessed with a very good life. Not like winning-the-lottery lucky, *better!*

I am the oldest in a family of nine. My parents loved each other and all of us. We were encouraged to explore, share, and work. Then I found the perfect life partner at an early age. With little money or liking for fancy dinner/movie/nightclub dates, we spent hours walking and sharing our hopes, plans, and dreams. I yearned to somehow become known as an artist. I was given one request: "Do whatever you like, but be home for the children." My husband always was encouraging of my artwork. He became my best, helpful, and most thoughtful critic. In return, I tried to always earn enough every year from sales of my artwork to at least cover my materials and not be a drain on the household accounts.

Thanks to this, I have felt supported and free enough over the years to go for a variety of things. I am not the type to stay home all day and do housework or watch the soaps. I started my career at Vermont Public Radio (VPR). Bless them! They were happy to have volunteers, even if they brought along toddlers.

Then, back to Connecticut, where our life got twisted when my husband was hit head-on in a car accident just months before we were to build our first house. I had to grow up, be the rock of the family for a while as he coped with pain and reevaluating our plans. Instead of doing the "sweatless" jobs of chasing permits, ordering supplies, and vetting our few contractors, I became actively involved in construction. I learned rough plumbing, wiring, carpentry. Over the years I went on to do all the insulating, roof installation, stuccoing, tilework and most of the painting on all our buildings.

Once my children went back to school, I had a huge chunk of free time. I became a substitute teacher and went to college, acquiring my associate's degree. As a substitute and confirmed space exploration believer, I was able to tap into the education mandate of NASA and signed up for their Lunar Sample course. That culminated months later in a whirlwind week bringing the program to our school district in Connecticut, lecturing to about fifteen hundred children in a five-day period. It was very cool to have the local bank open up early each morning for little ol' me to get the metal Lunar Sample case from their vault. My husband just likes to refer to me as a NASA-certified *lunatic!*

We became actively involved in Scouting. We have been leaders, assistant leaders, committee member, merit badge consultants. Many friends of all ages were made along the way, and we have hosted and been hosted by Scouters from several other countries. Somewhere along the way, I found myself gradually accumulating a collection of Girl Scout (and some International Scout) memorabilia, and so I continue to be a volunteer to this day in Girl Scouts; no longer as a leader, but as a historian/archivist/lecturer.

Due to my husband's injuries, we moved to Florida. When tornadoes hit Osceola County, my experience as an artist repairing and working with archival media proved to be helpful skill when organizing the sorting and stabilization of damaged paper goods (photos, documents, etc.) blown into the swamps by the storms.

Once the children grew, with the help of family and friends we remodeled our second home (and former airplane hangar), out on a grass strip airport. It is an ongoing joint sculpture project. I have handmade tiles for it using over three tons of clay, and opened up the interior by painting the walls and ceiling as a sky. The 40' by 12' hangar door is a life-sized mural of the plane my husband is building. A fine woodworker, he is gradually doing all the cabinets and interior trim in cypress, cedar and a palette of other woods. I say gradually, because five years ago we began trying to live in two places at once!

My husband became a contract engineer, and although our home remains in Florida, we also have an apartment in Georgia. We commute, spending as much of our free time as we can at our home base in Florida. My solo projects and volunteer work (with local Girl Scouts on a G.S. history in Florida, for example) can lead to more time spent in one place or the other. Fortunately for us, our son also stays at the Florida house for his job working construction, so it is usually occupied. Soon we hope to be there pretty much full-time, but anything can happen!

Although contract engineering was an exciting opportunity for my husband, I was at a loss. I was looking for a new direction to take my artwork, as well as something to fill my time.

The latter was easy. Savannah is where Girl Scouts U.S.A. (GSUSA) was founded in 1912, and when I was in town a few years before marketing my Girl Scout poster, a local staff member asked for my help. She was in charge of the Girl Scout First Headquarters, which is a small museum left to the local girls by Juliette Low. "If you are ever in Savannah," she had told me, "would you please come and help organize our uniform collection."

All that was good, but I have an addictive hunger to create. The challenge was to come up with something I could do that would be a series, marketable in more places than Georgia or Florida, watercolors (due to living in an apartment), and that I would enjoy doing.

The historic section of Savannah is a stroller's delight. Interesting architecture, patchwork pavement punctuated by delightful squares of live oaks and flowering shrubbery abound. Sidewalks abut ivy covered, mossy old brick or stucco-faced walls that hide secret little gardens. The only glimpse to the passerby is often through a charming wrought iron gate.

Gradually, the idea dawned that gates would be an interesting theme for a series. I set a goal of twenty-four to keep motivated. Since I hope eventually to exhibit the collection outside of Savannah, I began to collect little tidbits about the gates, the building it went with, or the area nearby. One day while out walking, I was bemoaning the eventual breakup of the set of paintings. My husband suggested I gather it all into a book. I approached a young local historian about writing it, and she was interested. My life whenever I was in Savannah settled into a routine of about 30 hours a week volunteering at First Headquarters, and early mornings, nights and alternate weekends painting (we are back to no TV in Georgia—it is too distracting!).

After about six months I had over a baker's dozen of watercolors, but lost my writer. My husband wouldn't let the idea die, and urged (prodded, nagged...) me to continue with the writing as well as the artwork. Eighteen or so done, and the publisher who was interested had to back out due to illness.

My husband refused to let me give up the book idea, and in an amazing leap of faith in my talent and ability, offered to underwrite the publishing cost. He began researching online for options and found a good print-on-demand site.

With twenty-five gates, a map, and one more that I just *had* to paint, he got an opportunity to work back in Florida where we could live full-time at home again. But I was not allowed to quit on the book! With my son's assistance on the computer layout and his friend's connection to upload the massive file on a high-speed connection (for a bottle of Everclear!), the deed was done.

Now I faced the challenge of marketing a Savannah book from Vero Beach, Florida. It was a delightful role reversal to take my husband on a business trip to Savannah.

Within a year, the Florida job was over so we opted to go back to Georgia. But this time I had a fabulous reason to be here: my book had been picked up by a "real" publisher, The History Press. Someone in Savannah had seen my book and passed it on to them, suggesting it would make an interesting pocket guide book.

As I write this, the first edition of my book, *Gates of Savannah,* has sold out. My publisher is looking for a printer for a second edition, as the original printer has gone out of business. I have learned not to worry too much about what is next in life, because something interesting has always turned up. For instance, in the summer of 2009 I was given my first opportunity to be a professional guest lecturer at a convention.

My artwork runs through a variety of subject matter: gates, aviation, dragons, Scouting, orchids; and an array of media: pen & ink, watercolors, acrylics, oils, ceramic, and mixed (a.k.a. whatever it takes to get the result I desire).

My second book, *Juliette Gordon Low and Historic Georgia,* a coloring/history book, was just printed. Life is full of excitement and surprises when you reach for the tantalizing goals.

Loving to Listen
Paige P. Fortner

Paige Fortner works at a hair salon with large windows overlooking a canal to Florida's Intracoastal Waterway, a view full of tall grasses, native birds, palm trees and sunshine. It is only fitting that her passion for cutting and styling hair would also demand the discovery of a beautiful environment in which to perform her job. Paige is one of those rare people you meet whose influence extends far beyond her function. To put it in a Zen way, her work is with form but the result goes beyond form.

As I sit and enjoy another beautiful weekend away in Key West, my own paradise, I realize that none of this would be possible if I hadn't made the choice to follow my heart and do what I love to do for a living…hair. I was one of the lucky ones who knew exactly what I wanted to do when I grew up. I just didn't know how much joy it would bring to my life.

As a kid growing up in the seventies with naturally curly hair, I had so many bad experiences trying to get my out-of-control locks to look like the pictures I saw on posters and in magazines. I think the hardest part was that no one would listen to me about how much it would shrink, frizz, and absolutely freak out if it were not cut to just the right length. All the family photos and school pictures serve as an added reminder as to how bad it really was. Finally, at the age of thirteen, I met a hair stylist who took the time to listen, and I got a great haircut that I could actually work with. That opened my eyes to the fact that if you just take the time to listen to people, you can find out what problems they are having and help them work their way through them. It seemed simple enough.

If you talk to 100 different hair stylists you will get 100 different answers as to why we do what we do. There are thousands of us out there, and this profession can offer you as much or as little as you want. We range from the very top in our field to the ones who only go to their jobs every day because they have to. I like to think that the only difference in all of us is passion for what we do and why we do it. After twenty-three years of "standing behind a chair" and working on countless numbers of people, I can honestly say I love what I do for a living. I only went into it with the thought that I would listen to what each person had to say and try to help them achieve their goals; but what I have found is that I have gotten as much fulfillment as, I hope, I have given to my customers throughout this journey.

As hair stylists, we are some of the few people you will allow to touch you. Think about it… How many people, let's say strangers, do you let touch you and rub their hands through your hair for any period of time? Not many! As a result I have had the advantage of learning so much about people and their lives. Everyone has a story and you can grow from each experience you share with them. Some people only come to maintain their look, others need another person's opinion, some need a neutral party to talk to, and some just need someone to listen, while others know what they want and just need help to achieve their visual goals. Because everyone is so different, I have had to open my mind and hear what they say so I can help them to realistically achieve their desires.

In return I have had the opportunity to learn so much about people and what interests them. They have shared their experiences with me and I have grown as a person. I have found that no matter what it is you want to know, if you ask enough people you encounter in your day you will get your answer. Who needs the Internet or a newspaper? Go to work at a hair salon! Keep it professional! Gossiping is not cool! Needless to say, I have learned to become a chameleon in order to work with so many different personalities.

A person's hairstyle is the only accessory, other than a wedding ring, that you wear every single day. It can be worn any way between casual and formal. It's a "style"; it changes daily. Whether it's good or bad, it definitely affects how you feel about yourself. A really bad hair day can make you just want to crawl back in bed and forget about all of your responsibilities; it can make that beautiful gown not so pretty. But a good hair day — WOW! The sun shines brighter, you walk a little taller, and for however long it lasts, life just seems a little easier. Use your hair to express yourself. Change it depending on your mood. If it doesn't do exactly what you want that day, don't worry. Tomorrow you have another chance.

If you are fortunate enough to recognize what you want to do with your life, take all the steps to learn to be the absolute best you can be. Appreciate every moment you get to spend doing it and it really seems as if you're not working. Sure, there are days I would like to stay at home, but once I get behind that chair it just takes me over. I get to listen, share my talent, and in return the whole world is opened up for me to see.

LOVE WHAT YOU DO AND THE REWARDS WILL FOLLOW AND THEN MAYBE YOU CAN SPEND SOME EXTRA TIME IN YOUR OWN PARADISE.

I've listened, I've touched, and boy have I learned! Thank you so much to all of the amazing people who have allowed me to be a part of their lives even for only a few precious minutes.

But You Don't *Look* Like a Warden
Pamela K. Withrow

Pamela K. Withrow grew up on a farm in Indiana, received her higher education in Michigan, and became the first female Warden in the 115-year history of the Michigan Reformatory prison. Her story is one of determination and accomplishment. Along the way she turned heartache into happiness and fear into a fire to succeed. I only met her once, but she left a lasting impression.

"But you don't *look* like a warden." I used to get that a lot when I told strangers what I had been doing for a living since I was thirty-two years old. Because while I was a sturdy woman, I looked more like the English teacher I'd intended to become than someone who should be running a prison. Why the career change? Poverty. Yes, it was simple poverty that led me into the field of Corrections, but it was love for the work that kept me there for twenty-five years.

Nothing in my early life suggested I'd end up running a series of prisons for adult men. The Indiana farm where I grew up was home to my grandparents, my parents, a great-aunt and three younger sisters, as well as a host of cats and our cash crops of hogs and cattle. We raised most of the food for ourselves and the animals, and made most of our own clothes. So we were far from rich, but we had a large extended family and church and school friends to keep us company.

Everything changed when my parents made the decision to move to Haslett, Michigan. My father had a crop of four daughters and decided a new line of work was the only way to provide the college educations he thought were necessary to their continued livelihood. The move turned my life upside down. The social adjustment to a new school in my senior year proved very difficult, though I continued to do well academically. I also met the man who became the instrument of my impoverishment, and we dated most of that year until I left for Michigan State University, where I'd been accepted into the Honors College. MSU was a few short miles from Haslett, but a universe away from the family life I had known.

My first year of college nearly destroyed me. Dorm life was not farm life, and I encountered people and experiences, from resentful roommates to dangerous pranks, that I could not overcome. Unable to handle this dark set of circumstances on my own, I returned home to my parents and the comfortable dating relationship I had enjoyed with my high school boyfriend. By spring I was pregnant, married, and on my way to a divorce and the welfare rolls.

It was really the birth of my son and the unreliability of his father that pushed me back into school. Enrolling at Lansing Community College, I worked full-time as a telephone operator while carrying a full load of classes. I also learned about LEAP, a federal program designed to improve the caliber of police officers by providing tuition and other support for law enforcement studies. Under this program I would have books and tuition paid for if I agreed to work in law enforcement for four years after college. So I developed a burning desire to become a cop.

When I returned to Michigan State, I was counseled that I was too bright and idealistic to become a police officer (I later realized this really meant *too female*) and it was suggested that perhaps I should consider law school. MSU created some barriers for entry into the Criminal Justice program, so I changed my major to pre-law, but kept taking a few law enforcement classes and graduated in 1975. Then the University of Michigan in Ann Arbor accepted me into their Law School. However, with a young son, denial of further support from Social Services, and no provision for part-time law students, I was forced to leave the program. I returned to the Lansing area to look for work. Remembering my commitment to work four years in law enforcement or start paying back book and tuition money, I looked into that field and discovered an opportunity with the Michigan Department of Corrections (MDOC) minimum security camp headquarters. Ingham County had continued me on their welfare caseload and another federal program (WIN) offered to pay my salary for six months if an employer would agree to hire me. Since the camp program was chronically under funded, they were delighted to get a free worker. The camp headquarters superintendent later confided to me that he hadn't intended to keep me around when my unpaid stint ended. Apparently my work was good enough because, instead, he offered me a classified civil service job and I was on my way to becoming a warden.

Within two years, I was running one of the camps (my first "first woman" job with the MDOC), which gave me more than three years of preparation for moving up to a secure prison. When the Corrections Department experienced riots at the three major penitentiaries, my tranquil period as camp supervisor ended. I was transferred to Jackson Prison, first as the administrative assistant to the warden and then as the housing deputy for seven cell blocks housing 2,800 prisoners, including two units of segregation—one for inmates needing protection and the other for management/security problem prisoners.

This was really baptism by fire. Jackson was the world's largest walled prison and a management and control nightmare. The riots had started when staff tried to lock down the prison without the warden's authorization. There was no trust among the three key groups at the facility. The staff felt the administrators didn't have any concern about their safety and security needs; prisoners, who knew the custody staff had acted without management approval and thus were wary of all officers; and administrators, who had just had the worst possible thing happen: they had lost control of the facility, resulting in staff and prisoner injuries and millions of dollars in physical plant damage. This had happened because of a breakdown in relations between line staff and management.

The brief time in the warden's office was high pressure and required long hours as MDOC, media, and legislative inquiries were handled and interminable meetings were held to determine both the causes for the riot and how Jackson would operate in the future. But that job was easy compared to that of housing deputy (another "first woman" assignment). After a few weeks, I was in MDOC Director Perry Johnson's office in tears.

Perry patted me on the shoulder and sent me back to prison with the advice, "Nobody has ever been able to do that job. Just do the best you can." A second visit a few weeks later resulted in the same response.

I knew I needed to find another way out. I applied for, and was accepted into, a two-year appointment with the National Academy of Corrections in Longmont, Colorado. Although my application had been approved by Director Johnson's office, when I applied for a release date it was denied. Suddenly I knew how a prisoner feels when his parole is canceled! My son's visions of skiing in the Rockies and my own desire for new challenges vanished as I was told that I was needed in Michigan.

What I *didn't* know was that I was slated to be named the first woman in Michigan to head a prison housing adult male offenders. I started at the medium security Michigan Dunes Correctional Facility on Valentine's Day in 1983, but it was not a loving reception that I received. The deputy warden at the facility thought he should have had my job and made it clear that I would receive no cooperation from him! Refusing to set myself up for failure so easily, I arranged a swap with another warden so that the deputy got a small promotion and I got a new deputy to train. The departing warden had also taken a number of supervisors to staff his newly opened facility, so I was able to hire many of the facility's managers and supervisors. I encouraged them to run the place by showing respect for both staff and offenders.

The brief stint at Jackson had convinced me that I never wanted a disturbance at any facility for which I was responsible. That meant paying close attention to the three "legs" necessary for facility balance. First, supervisors needed to listen to staff and prisoners and respond to their legitimate concerns while operating a safe, clean and secure facility. Second, staff who worked directly with offenders needed to serve as role models and share information accurately both with management and prisoners while enforcing rules uniformly. Finally, prisoners needed to feel safe and be able to earn and receive respect while being offered opportunities to change.

This sounds simple, but it takes a lot of attention to detail to be sure the "legs" stay balanced. Custody staff generally want security concerns to be the highest priority while prisoners want more freedom and activities. Supervisors can become office-bound while attending to paperwork, e-mail and phone calls; and fail to personally visit their areas of responsibility. The warden's job is to keep all the elements of the operation in balance, to motivate staff to serve the taxpayers by operating an excellent facility, and to encourage prisoners to take advantage of program opportunities so that they can become good neighbors when released from prison.

At the Dunes, this presented few challenges because the staff had a great work ethic, offenders were at a relatively low security level, and they were motivated to earn parole and go home. My comfort zone was short-lived, however, as less than four years later Director Bob Brown offered me the challenge of running the Michigan Reformatory in Ionia. This facility was one of the three old, walled prisons involved in the 1981 riots, and I'd already done more time than I cared to at Jackson right after those events. But no woman had ever been given a chance to run one of Michigan's major penitentiaries, and I wanted that opportunity. My son was studying at the University of Michigan and I had only myself to consider. In July of 1986 I moved.

I had a personal motivation to be closer to Lansing, as this change allowed me to marry the love of my life. We exchanged vows in the parlor of a house adjacent to the prison where I had an apartment and where I lived for that first year as the Reformatory's warden.   My husband visited on Wednesday nights and I went home on weekends. Not an ideal arrangement for newlyweds, but conditions at the facility were so dismal that I hadn't the energy for a two-hour commute on top of the twelve and fourteen-hour days I was putting in.

This time I was prepared for the deputy's hostility and was not at all disappointed when the previous warden took him and other supervisors with him to his new job in Jackson. But interviewing for my new deputy I was faced with a new dilemma: the best candidate was another woman.   Now, I'd observed a pattern of pairings for wardens and deputies in our agency and, while the norm was still two white males, the usual variation was white/minority or male/female.   If I hired my preferred candidate, the MDOC would have two women running a high security prison, one a minority. I thought this required a check-in with Director Bob Brown, who is, in fact, quite black.

When I explained the issue, Brown just smiled and said, "Well, we've run these places for a lot of years with two men; I don't see how this is any different." What a great response, and a challenge to me to be stronger about my conviction that women were fully capable of working in male facilities.

After fifteen years I retired from the Reformatory. We had exited a Federal Consent Decree* that came out of those riots in 1981, become accredited by the American Correctional Association, and started the MDOC on the road to evidence-based programming with offerings in cognitive restructuring, skill training and problem-solving.

So, what was it like to be the first woman in all these jobs? Scary, exciting, rewarding and exhausting—sometimes all at once. Probably the most disconcerting aspect of being named the "first woman," whether camp supervisor or warden, was the media attention. The MDOC offered some training in this area, but I wasn't prepared for the kinds of questions and the requests for photos these appointments prompted.

For example, I posed with the camp dog, a nice beagle, when the *Brighton Argus* did a story about the new Camp Brighton supervisor. What I hadn't thought about was the liability that dog presented for visitors and the outcry from staff when my bosses saw the story and ordered the dog off the premises. (I never told those bosses the dog was one of a pair and that we also had a litter of puppies in the garage.) I learned to say no to the press and sometimes to answer the question I wanted them to ask instead of the one they did.

A bigger issue for me, however, was the pressure to succeed. I knew if I failed it would delay opportunities for the many qualified women entering the field and that, conversely, my success would accelerate hiring and promotion for females. One key to survival was the support of my female colleagues. In fact, during those awful times at Jackson, four of us met monthly to exchange information, prop each other up, and just laugh or cry as the occasion demanded. That networking became so important that we encouraged other women to form similar support groups and would travel to their facilities to help them begin the process. In addition, I joined professional organizations and went to conferences to shore up my professional identity and to stay current.

Family was another element that helped me stay balanced. My son laughingly referred to me as, "my mom, the warden," and my husband, who was retired during most of my time at the Reformatory, took on many of the household responsibilities. We also traveled extensively, as I believed that a warden's absence is important for staff development. Prisons are pretty resilient and often manage to endure even with poor management, but the person at the helm does make a difference. I would like to think the ones I managed became better for it, and that some of the improvements were due to the humanizing gender perspective I may have brought to the job, but that is really for others to say.

Would I do it again or recommend someone take other "first woman" posts? You bet! If the field is one you love and you are up for the challenge, the rewards are well worth the risks. In my case, those rewards included being named to the Michigan Women's Hall of Fame, Michigan State University's Criminal Justice Wall of Fame, and selection as the North American Association of Wardens and Superintendent's Warden of the Year, as well as receipt of honorary doctorates from Grand

Valley State University and Ferris State University. Not a bad way for a farm girl from Indiana to end a career.

* A Federal Consent Decree was issued by the U.S. Department of Justice in 1984 as a result of inmate riots that occurred at the Michigan Department of Corrections Jackson prison complex in 1981. In order to be released from this mandate, the Federal Judge overseeing the consent decree has determined that the State has satisfied the requirements of the decree and all conditions have been met; and can thereby be released from supervision by the court.

Swimming in a Sea of Men

Pauline Nefcy

Pauline Nefcy and I went to a Catholic, all-girls high school in Detroit together. During those years she excelled at basketball, field hockey, driver's ed, partying, and academic studies; particularly math. Pauline is also a lifelong swimmer, and swimmers tend to be successful because they strive to do their personal best. She chose the male-dominated field of accounting, traveled extensively, and welcomed life's challenges. Our friendship has stood the test of time, as recently my husband and I attended the wedding of her eldest son, in the Seattle area where Pauline now makes her home. Here is her "fish story."

When I graduated with my M.B.A. and M.S. in Community Health in 1981, I decided that I wanted it all—family, career, friends, an exciting life. After graduating I worked at Ernst and Whinney, an accounting firm, in order to fulfill the requirements for my CPA. I had to keep my eyes on my target plan continually as I found myself in an occupation that was dominated by men. I was a small minnow learning to swim in a sea of sharks.

Some women were easily sidetracked by the mentality and behaviors of the men at that time; I found I needed to ignore the male coffee clique — the sexist comments, outright prejudice and general mean gossip — in order to keep focused. I had neither the time nor the energy to spend on their issues. Over the years, many valuable experiences taught me timeless skills needed to deal with men's attitudes toward women in the work force. I would like to share three of these experiences and lessons learned over a fifteen-year period. These actual events offer an historical perspective on the evolving role of women in business and the shift in men's attitudes as women became their bosses.

The year is 1985. I am the Assistant Director of Finance at Virginia Mason Hospital. I am very pregnant with my third child. My boss, Ray, is the Director of Finance, a wonderful man. I am hard working, creative, and receiving promotions and raises every six months. Hurray!! Of course, there is a lot of blather going on between the men at the water cooler. I am being called names such as aggressive, not a team player, etc. I hear the rumors, but since I am being so handsomely rewarded for my work, I continue to climb the ladder and ignore the chatter.

One day Ray asked me to sub for him at a breakfast meeting of all the local hospital finance directors. I knew all of the men, as they were members of Healthcare Financial Management Association, an organization in which I was actively involved. Ray told me that the meeting was at 7:30 a.m. at the Rainier Club.

The next morning my alarm wakes me at five. I fix breakfast for my two children, make their lunches, and deliver them to school and daycare. I grab my coffee and drive into Seattle. I am late for the meeting because I cannot find the Rainier Club (pre MapQuest). It seems to be hidden. At last I find the building, wander into the dark cave of an entryway and head for the receptionist. I am seven months pregnant, wearing the frilly maternity clothes that were the only fashion available at the time. I am carrying a briefcase, exhausted from my search and showing it. The receptionist looks surprised to see me as I explain that I am looking for the breakfast meeting. She appears to be considering what to do with me.

Finally she sends me on my way. I start down a long, dark, quiet hallway. As I move down the hall, I peer at professional pictures of elderly, distinguished-looking men, commemorating past presidents of the Rainier Club. The men are all posed in business suits with intimidating looks on their faces. From my perspective they look old and very unhappy (maybe they were happy earlier in their lives). As I continue down the hall, a thought comes to me — *am I in an all-male club?* Perhaps that is why the men in the pictures look so unhappy. I had heard that these clubs existed but was always puzzled as to why one would attend a male-only club. I find females are much more fun.

As I come to the designated door I hesitate. If this is a strictly men's organization as it seems apparent, women are surely not allowed in this part of the club. Why did the receptionist allow me to travel down this hallway? After some thought, she must have figured I was the secretary who was delivering some papers to my boss (later I discovered that this was indeed her thinking). But I have a meeting to attend, so at 7:45 I open the door. The twelve men at the table look up in surprise, not knowing quite what to do next. After a few awkward moments, Bob invites me to sit down at the table with them and they continue their meeting.

I felt a little blindsided by the meeting at the gentlemen's club. I never understood why Ray (a wonderful man?) sent me to the meeting at a club that did not welcome — or allow — ladies. Maybe he knew I would not attend the meeting if I knew about the Rainier Club. I never did ask Ray why he placed me in this situation; some things you do not want answers to as you may not like the answer or you may need to respond. Secretly, knowing that I may have been the first woman to attend a meeting behind those closed doors did please me.

As an addendum, it is my understanding that the Rainier Club, similar to Rotary, now accepts women as members. During the 1990s, when many young males did not want to join men-only clubs, membership in these clubs declined and they were forced to accept females in order to survive financially. It always comes down to money.

Let's fast forward to 1990. Jim, my husband, and I are living in Clyde Hill, Washington, raising our three children and enjoying successful careers. Jim works for Arthur Andersen (AA) in the consulting area and I am working at Group Health Cooperative (GHC) as the Director of Decision Support. Group Health is the largest HMO in the state of Washington.

Life is good, both companies are flush with cash, and we are enjoying ourselves. There are many parties and retreats sponsored by AA. For years we enjoyed Christmas parties, summer barbeques, company retreats, beach picnics. Every month there was a company affair to attend, with lots of food, drinks and dancing. I always had a good time with Jim at these events.

At the time, only men were promoted to the management level at AA. The wives did not work, talked about shopping and spending money on credit cards. I was not considered good partner wife material, as I did not meet their criteria; and to make matters worse, I had a different last name. To avoid addressing me by my correct name, if there was a need to catch my attention, the men would try to make eye contact, but quickly resorted to calling me "hey you."

By 1990, I was in a position to hire and fire consultants, influence which accounting firms were hired, propose large information system projects, and recommend consulting firms for these projects — firms such as Arthur Andersen. One day one of Jim's peers, let's call him Pete, met with Jim and asked if Jim could introduce him to his wife (me). Pete had recently received a promotion and was on track for partnership if he could sell consulting work. We had seen Pete at these functions and parties for years; in fact, I think he addressed me by "hey you" a few times. Jim told him that he was eight years too late. For eight years men like Pete had the opportunity to develop me as a client. After years of being called "hey you," I chose to run away from people like Pete. My only regret is that I didn't run away from them years earlier.

Let's jump to 1995. Barb (Assistant Controller at Group Health) and I (Director of Decision Support) are attending the Annual Healthcare Financial Management meeting. At this meeting there is a vendor show that consists of 300+ vendors with the newest ideas and products in healthcare accounting systems, medical record systems and claims systems. We always like to spend time viewing the newest system developments and products and bring our findings back to Group Health management. It takes most of the afternoon to view all the products.

One of Barb's employees, Tim, is attending the conference and joins us as we move purposefully from booth to booth. Tim is a tall (over 6′4″), handsome 33-year-old and he is very pleased to be able to join us. This is Tim's opportunity to discuss issues with us and be able to know us on an individual basis — a great opportunity for a person at his level.

As we enter the first booth, Tim attracts the vendors like a magnet. They give Tim their sales pitch and he gives them his business card. Barb and I are busy picking up brochures, pens and other items the vendors are giving away. In one of the booths we pick up a couple of plastic bags to carry all of our goodies and information. Barb and I are both carrying two fairly full plastic bags. Booth after booth, Tim attracts the vendors and we continue to pick up the information.

After a while, we lose Tim as the vendors continue to talk to him and we are moving faster in order to view all of the booths. Tim finally catches up to us and looks rather sheepish. He tells us that it has dawned on him that these vendors think he is the boss and we are his assistants carrying around his bags. He would like to set the record straight and let us know that he was not trying to upstage us. We replied, "We know the vendors thought we were your secretaries. You did us a favor as you will be the one the vendors will be contacting, not us. We just wanted to be able to review all their current information without being harassed."

Some things change and some things stay the same. In the eyes of many men and women, even in the mid-nineties, a tall handsome man must be the boss and the women with him must be his secretaries.

I started my journey thirty years ago. I learned to be a very good swimmer and grew to be a good-size fish. The perceived value of women in society and the workplace has come a long way. There are now many female fish helping each other learn to swim in a sea of men, and the lessons from my experiences may no longer be relevant. However, if you find yourself in a situation where you perceive you are being treated as a minnow by the sharks in your pond, remember the lessons I learned through the experiences shared here: don't ask why—you may not like the answer and may need to act on it; run—change positions or group—these men are not going to change their attitudes; and use such men's ignorance to your advantage.

Know when you've learned what you can from a situation and recognize when it's time to walk away. "Knowledge is power" is an old adage that still holds true today. My advice to you is to use your priceless time working smart, acting professionally, being a value-added person to your company, and seeking promotions and opportunities, and the day will come when *you* are the boss.

Untitled Kidnapping Essay

Rachel Raines

Rachel Raines sought refuge at my home in the Blue Ridge Mountains of North Carolina, along with my son, for a brief time after the robbery and kidnapping described here. The story is told in the language and cadence of the young, with a bit of the slightly crazed rambling style reminiscent of Hunter S. Thompson and a touch of old Hollywood film noir. Rachel didn't want to be melodramatic. In fact, her story is a sound lesson in how a talent for acting turned into a skill that helped save her life.

It was a small car; one of those two-door designs with a low ceiling. Dark both inside and out, it made the space seem even smaller in the absence of light. With the exception of the dashboard lights, glowing dark blue and so tiny they didn't even illuminate the lettering above each one stating their invisible purposes, everything was dark. There was a brand new GPS stuck right in the middle of the car, too big to move your legs around, not that I would have. I was barely breathing. Small spaces always made me nervous. I wouldn't have liked that car no matter the situation, but I *really* didn't like it that night.

There were three men in the car with me, overcrowding the already cramped space. One window, the one on my passenger side in the back seat, was cracked about an inch. We had been driving for so long; indefinitely it seemed, in real time only a few hours. But parked now, the men accompanying me had produced a pipe, and smoke inhaled and exhaled from the window opening as the men took turns pulling throaty bubbling breaths of crack rock, one after another, each release crackling more than the last like water hitting hot asphalt on a summer afternoon. It was three hours into one of the most terrifying nights of my life, the night three crackheads broke into my boyfriend's apartment, robbing us both as well as his roommate. In the final seconds they decided to take me as hostage and held me at gunpoint as they left. Which is how I ended up inhaling secondhand crack smoke in this tiny car and convincing myself that if they were going to rape or kill me they would have done so immediately.

I just had to keep playing along.

Ironically, I moved to LA from my home in St. Louis to pursue an acting career. Like most every other aspiring actress in Hollywood, I was waitressing and sharing an apartment with a girlfriend. My roles thus far had been limited to local ads and bit parts in plays. Being petite with long blond hair, small voiced but capable of a piercing scream, I was perfect for the Victim at Halloween haunted houses and seasonal gigs at Disney. I was twenty but easily played younger. Little did I know my acting would help save my life.

It was an unusual night; it happened in real time and to the pace of many prior evenings spent in the company of friendly men. The offering of drugs, albeit strange, seemed to be a partial plea—their need to be absolved of the sins they committed by taking me, as though my forgiveness made a "situation normal" of the entire night. So, on the surface I forgave. I laughed at their jokes, watched the videos they showed me on the iPhone the driver held toward my face. I listened to them all examine their new treasures, snickering at the music on the stolen iPods they explored like children on Christmas morning. I felt the need to urinate, again, but since they had once released me from the vehicle, standing a few feet away and allowing me to pee in a darkened front yard, I felt my chances of mercy twice were slim. I breathed steadily and continued on into the night that became a showcase of lies.

It was difficult to remain convincing while I was thinking of jumping from the vehicle. To stop myself from following that impulse took all my will power and concentration. I nodded along to the smiling man holding the gun beside me, avoided watching the butcher knife in the door pocket as he told things I could not begin to hear. Instead, I heard the roar of blood pumping in my ears as it pounded to an alarming beat.

It is also hard to explain here the importance and purpose of the lies told that night. Not every one was spoken, nor were those spoken any more than pure luck on my part in thinking of them when I did. And I don't know if I can even call them lies. It was more of a performance. My role? Appealing to the whims of unstable armed men who terrified me.

I had to become someone else. I could not let them see my fear. I could not let them know the real me. I have some skill as an actress, but to say a particular talent was why I didn't die that night would be an exaggeration. What I knew upon entering that car was the same thing I know now, ultimately and without a doubt in my mind: those men did not *want* to kill me. I just had to continue to find a way of convincing them they didn't *have* to kill me either.

At some point things began to deteriorate. We had been driving around for hours. I had been acting like their best friend or a younger sister out for a joyride. Maybe I started to believe it. But the belief was only in my role, the part I played in what was beginning to be a very long play. At some point, the driver mentioned that "they did not hurt women." Yes, here we all were, full of respect for one another. Fear was fading fast. I began to feel that I would not be harmed, but I could not even begin to relax. How long would this last? Would I be taken somewhere indefinitely? Was anyone looking for me? Was this act going to go on forever? Finally, would they buy the ruse that I had to be at work for a telemarketing firm at 6 a.m.?

Looking back on it, the fact that they actually bought that I wasn't planning on immediately calling the police after my release absolutely baffles me. Perhaps giving the driver my real phone number when he asked, knowing he would quickly call my cell phone to check it, gave me that final edge of credibility. I cannot pretend that the copious amount of drugs being consumed didn't have something to do with it as well. When they were "kind" enough to give me my cell phone back, not turning it on gained me a certain level of trust. When they stopped the car several times, to buy drugs and throw out stolen goods with identifying marks and transfer me from the back to front seat, I am certain not running kept me from getting shot.

These men had to be comfortable enough to believe that letting me go wouldn't lead to their detriment. And I talked and lied and laughed until they believed that. I treated them with the casual attention one would show an overly friendly store clerk. I spoke to them politely, flirtatiously, with the casual mentioning of a boyfriend and the hunched posture of a too-young girl. These men were bad, not evil. There is a fine line between liking a girl...and wanting her.

Their behavior that night came from many different sources, some of which I am sure were habit and necessity (the drugs, the weapons, etc.), but seemed to lead only to underlying layers of guilt. Guilt that when toyed with could lead to resentment for those who made them feel the guilt to begin with; but when coddled, guilt that could be turned into feelings of validation for their actions. Beyond all the analysis, the less guilty my lies made them feel, the less they worried about the repercussions of letting me go.

This story is anticlimactic. These guys treated me as a casual acquaintance, a new friend, until the very moment of my release (with no sense of comprehension or concern for the real life from which they had stolen me). Each goodbye was spoken with a tone of fondness, and as they turned the corner of the street where I was released, I didn't see a head turn to look back. There was no warning or threat in the end, of pain that would come if I spoke to anyone. I was asked where I lived and lied once again, giving them an old address far from my current home. It was programmed into the GPS and I was driven there. When they were gone I rang a former neighbor's bell until he answered and called the police. One of the men activated the

GPS on a stolen phone and less than twenty-four hours later the three were caught, the police led right to them by the instrument of their folly. The driver of the car, the wielder of the gun and knife, was sentenced to twenty-five years in prison and the second man was sentenced to sixteen. The third man, having never entered the apartment or touched me, was not arrested.

I'm sure if you're looking for a moral you could find one. Keeping calm and level-headed in a dangerous situation obviously helped me quite a bit. It is easily a metaphor for many things. But what I really take away from the ordeal (besides how incredibly lucky I am that these specific men were so easily manipulated) is something that I think will stick with me for the rest of my life, and strangely enough, something my mother said to me casually many years ago. And that is, simply, you would be shocked what people can live through. Not just survive. But continue to live.

It was a small car.

It was a dark night in LA.

I am one strong dame.

Change of Course

Rebecca Stimson

Becky Stimson has been a friend since we worked together as college students at a downtown bookstore a block from the State Capitol in Lansing, Michigan. She had straight reddish hair she would tame with a sweep of her hand, and a straight face that easily broke into laughter she didn't bother to tame. Becky lived on a farm on the outskirts of town, with dear parents who reminded me of Mr. and Mrs. Santa Claus. I hailed from the city and she from the country, but we shared a love of books and writing that lasts to this day. In 2006 Rebecca Stimson established Clarkwood Connect LLC, continuing the work she had been engaged in for twenty years. As a personal historian, writer, editor, and group facilitator, her passion is "to make your voice heard." Now it's time to hear her voice.

One of my early childhood memories is of the oracle by which I thought I would live: the pink birthday candle. Certain years had little decals, pictures of the prophecy. At six a tricycle, at eight a bike, at eighteen a diploma, at twenty-one wedding rings. Each year around my birthday when the candle made its appearance, I stared at that timeline of my life and imagined getting the bike, and the diploma, and finally as presaged, reaching the pinnacle at the base of the candle: the rings. I had no expectations about what happened after that; I just thought my life would follow the course to a wedding at twenty-one.

It didn't. I am not married. Never have been.

My great expectations grew from my pretty idyllic family life: my brother, me, and two loving and supportive parents who exemplified the perfect match. Not perfect in the no flaws sense but in the I-married-the-love-of-my-life sense. They presented an enviable model of marriage with their respect, communication, compromise, and affection. It was to be desired, and I desired it.

The perfect match. For years I worried about it, searched for it, waited for it. Oh, to have that time and energy back or to have directed it toward a doctorate or training to swim across Lake Michigan!

I've always loved men and enjoyed their company. I adored my father and did everything I could to be interesting to my older brother. Ultimately I learned how to talk with boys and be their friend. In the '70s, one often read that successful romantic relationships began as friendships. I began to expect that is how it would happen for me. I had several fun and rewarding friendships with boys well into my twenties. We could talk about anything—including their girlfriends. Eventually they all married other women, and one came out of the closet.

A friend I dated in high school used to call me after he was divorced. He spoke matter-of-factly about his failed marriages. I lamented never finding The One. "You always got everything you wanted," he said. "If you'd really wanted to be married, you would be married."

That comment still rings in my ears.

At the time I still held some hope that He would come along. Now I know I was premenopausal and still prime for nesting.

A psychic once told me, "He will find you." I believed her. But I also knew from a fortune cookie that "If you're waiting for your ship to come in, you must first row out to meet it." So I thought I was responsible for helping him find me. After all, I knew women who had checked out the boats in the harbor, found the one they wanted to board, and wound up on deck. That wasn't my way. I thought friends might introduce me to appropriate prospects. I took a few interesting evening college classes where I thought I might meet some eligible men. I've worked on the shores of a seemingly endless pool of eligible bachelors: in bookstores and at a community college. Other colleagues in both places were finding their ships. I did not. In the early '90s, I decided a larger pool might help, so I joined a dating service to find someone compatible. When the fourth set-up turned out to be with a man not yet divorced, I jumped ship.

I decided I was simply looking for a Chris-Craft in a rowboat world.

One friend says I missed the boat because I waited too long; I wasn't at the dock when the fleet came in. She is of the opinion —just like my pink birthday candle—that 21 is the optimum age for getting on board. That's when she sighted her ship and embarked, and it's a pattern her daughters are following.

When I was a child, the single older females in my life were the widowed grandmother, the elderly aunt, and the divorced godmother.

My widowed grandmother was strong and affectionate and was without my grandfather longer than she'd been with him. She worked only in the home, studying cooking before she married and setting a high standard for our eating habits. She lived with my aunt and her family and then with us.

We visited the independent elderly aunt at the Ohio family home where she lived alone —a stunning museum of doilies, vases, dark heavy furniture you sank into, and the blended bouquet of wooden floors, Ivory soap, and talcum. A famous author proposed to her. She declined; we know not why.

My godmother was a single parent. She was an administrator at the university and traveled all over the country. By herself. In the '50s and '60s. She was fascinating and adventurous. Eventually she met the love of her life, and they were married in Gibraltar when she was 62. It was pretty amazing at the time and amazes me still.

A change in the status quo took place in the '60s during my formative years. In our twenties, it was common to see *Our Bodies, Our Selves* on friends' bookshelves. Written by a women's collective, that book opened our eyes to health issues, our sexuality, and the changing role of women. We learned we had a choice. The knowledge didn't change our biology though. Our urges were still to couple, mate, and feather the nest. Until menopause. When female urges change.

I relinquished the dream of being wife and mother years ago. Probably during perimenopause. You don't really know until it's over, but it's likely that's when I altered my expectations.

I am now in my fifties and postmenopausal. I have many single female friends in the same stage of life. Some are divorced. Most of us are single by choice. Choice? Until recently, I would have disagreed. Now I know my urge to mate was subsiding when I was in my forties and being replaced by another: to focus on myself. I have *Women's Bodies, Women's Wisdom*, written by a postmenopausal female physician, to thank for really understanding The Change of Life. And it certainly is.

During my quest, several married women older than I told me wistfully they envied me my freedom. More than one told me if they had it to do over, they wouldn't. We didn't talk about whether they'd choose to have children again. One professional woman on her second marriage told me to get a dog instead. When I told her I already had one, she said, "Get another." I did. It isn't quite the same thing, but they eagerly go where I go and sleep where I sleep.

While discussing my singleness with the mother of a high school friend, she said, "You were busy living your life." I didn't realize it then, but I see it now. Conscious or not, I am the one who has chosen. Sometimes I wonder if I would have been a good partner and a good mother. Then the movie of my life spent nurturing, teaching, listening, grieving, laughing, sharing, worrying, working, growing, and changing plays; and I realize that I have given a lot of myself to many and received much in return.

Those of us without children have been able to take a job because it allowed us to follow our passions and quit a job because it was no longer fulfilling, a quality we think more about as we embrace The Change.

Holidays when married sisters are up to their eyebrows in preparations and accommodations can be a time of pampering and self-reflection for some of us. Most people cannot understand why we might prefer to be alone. When others are absorbed by family dynamics and expectations, the single woman listens to her music, watches her movies, cooks her favorite food, reads her favorite books, walks her beloved dogs, and thanks her lucky stars for the life she has created for herself.

I miss men. I enjoy their company and their point of view. I would really like to have more testosterone around, but it can be challenging for single women to have male friends. Women and men share many attributes, but we make different choices for many different reasons. For better or worse, richer or poorer, in sickness and in health, some of us are single and very content.

So what of the single woman's life? It is rich and diverse and full of choices regardless of one's hormonal stage. Ultimately our decisions have brought us to where we are whether we made them with only ourselves in mind or because we thought they would please someone else. Today the single woman is my friend, my cousin, my neighbor, my colleague. A student, a grandmother, a lawyer, an entrepreneur. Retired, unemployed, starting a new job, working 60 hours a week. We have children, dogs, cats, and as we embrace The Change, for many of us, a life largely of our choosing.

Who Said You Can't Hit a Home Run?
Sally Hall

When I asked Sally Hall to write something, I specifically had in mind the adoption of her two Native American children and how they thrived under the care of Sally and her good husband, John, a former friar. As so often happened in the writing of this book, her contribution was full of surprises, things of which I knew nothing. Sally came of age at a time when women had to struggle to be accepted and to achieve. Still, she managed to excel in business, sports, community service, and finally, motherhood. Sally approaches everything with patience, due diligence and skill. She enjoys hunting for treasure on the beach and also has an impressive collection of Indian arrowheads discovered along creek beds and forested lands. She plays a mean game of euchre and I love to partner with her against our husbands. We usually win. Just don't tell her she can't play ball.

The time was 7th grade. It was team tryouts. I was short, skinny, blond, and looked like a 4th grader. The coaches must have seen some potential in me, or — more likely — they were told to give a chance to those students who really wanted to play. At any rate, I made the All Star Baseball Team and spent most of my time sitting on the bench. I went to all the practices, did all the workouts with the team. But no one thought I could play, much less hit a home run.

During one game I was playing my usual position as bench warmer until the last inning. By that time the All Stars were way ahead so they put me in. I was pretty mad by then but decided to put my energy to good use. I hit a home run. Fact is, I hit the ball so far they couldn't find it. This was the beginning of many events in my life, my husband's life, and my children's lives when someone said no you can't, or even myself when I thought the same thing; but I encouraged everyone else that, yes, they can.

In school I did fairly well. Smart but not the smartest. Good enough to be awarded Best All-Round Student in academics and activities for the class of 1961. In college I hit the *Can't Do* wall again when told I would not return for a second semester of chemistry because the subject was for men only. Guess what, I returned for chemistry along with seven others. Two hundred and thirty-five women from that first semester moved on to other things, never to return. Today's female students probably find this hard to imagine. But the way was paved by women of my generation. The time was right, change was needed, and we took up the cause; first as individuals and then en masse.

Eventually I became the supervisor of the Chemistry Department at St. Elizabeth Hospital. Under my direction, the staff learned how to do things and do them well, and to become supervisors themselves. The work was fairly interesting and the hospital a good place to gain experience; but after fifteen years of low pay I was ready for a change.

As a sales rep for Union Carbide, I thoroughly enjoyed changing a very low-producing territory to the best in the country. When I was asked to join Instrumentation Lab selling lab equipment, I again took a low-producing territory to third in the nation, and I was inducted into their Presidents Club because of my success. I was driving a Corvette (another *"women can't do"* milestone), living in a riverfront condominium, earning a good living, and having a ball.

Success, however, is not just a lofty goal, a game of numbers, or a selfish effort at all costs to competitors. I genuinely wanted to help my customers, not just sell to them; and that is what made my work rewarding in so many ways. I took the time to teach them how to maintain their equipment, run different tests, even use some other company's products. Since I was always available to help, they started switching to my reagents. (A *reagent* is a substance or compound added to a system in order to bring about a chemical reaction or see if one occurs. When purchasing or preparing chemicals, *reagent-grade* describes chemical substances of sufficient purity for use in chemical reactions and physical testing.)

Large hospitals needed my assistance also. They knew how to do everything; however, when they couldn't get the service engineer they knew I would come in and help. They also knew, since I became a top rep, that I had the respect of my regional director and the corporate office, and that when I called them they would come down and do anything for my customers to make things right. I didn't have to call very often. So, success involves helping other people.

Finally, at thirty-seven, I got married. John Hall had been in the Franciscan Order for a decade. The last place he lived as a monk was Duns Scotus College in Southfield, Michigan, an Italian Gothic-style complex and school of philosophy for over 1,000 friars from 1930-1979. While there, he was always doing electrical, plumbing and boiler room maintenance. Eventually his talent for fixing things became clear, and he ended up running the physical plant for the entire monastery. John was one of hundreds of priests and other religious who left their orders during the turbulent '60s and '70s in the Catholic Church. He received a papal dispensation, releasing him from his vows of chastity, poverty and obedience. He was free to marry.

John was down-to-earth and sweet, and he had substance — the antithesis of the shallow men I had been dating. I was a nice Catholic gal who had never been married, and saw something in this guy. We were born within a week of one another. We were pretty happy to find each other.

Entering the state of wedded bliss a tad later than usual, my husband and I were ready to start a family. We tried to have children but were unsuccessful. We placed our name on an adoption agency list, but were told we were too old to adopt. In the state of Ohio no one over thirty-six can adopt a baby. Why? We were financially in good standing, physically in great shape, and loved children. This law seemed completely unfair. Then John was transferred to Texas, so my career came to an end and our hopes for adoption looked slim. However, as I always say, "God must have sent us to Texas," because two things happened. Really extraordinary.

First, I ran for City Council in Southlake, Texas. I ran because our neighborhood had insufficient water to take a shower or put out a fire. After repeated trips to City Council by our neighborhood, we were told they didn't have the money. I could not believe it. NO again. None of our neighbors had the time, but we decided the only way to get something done was for one of us to run for City Council. So I said I'd run. Now, bear in mind I am a Yankee, a woman, and I have only lived in the city for two years. No way did I expect to win. But I was going to make a lot of noise about our situation and I was just as qualified as anyone who was presently on the council. Well, guess what, I won. In two years I was able to be instrumental in bringing the City back. I served three terms on the Council and one term on the Zoning Board of Adjustments. On my volunteer time as a council member I heard many times *No, Mrs. Hall, we can't do that.* But we did, and everyone benefited from our insistence on quality regarding the development of Southlake.

I also worked closely with the oil tank farms and the local fire department to make certain the city had the necessary equipment to handle minor emergencies and worst-case scenarios, an issue that came to a head after 9/11, when cities began discussing in earnest how to protect citizens from potential dangers. I'm sure the tank farm owners were glad they had invested in safety features and plans ten years earlier. And I'll bet they never admitted that their first response was *No, it will never happen.*

The second extraordinary thing that occurred was that we were able to adopt our son, Bob, and eventually his sister, Jen. What a godsend! Bob was seven at the time and Jen a year younger. Neither of them could read and both suffered from malnutrition. They were from an abusive home and experienced problems associated with abandonment and neglect. We fed them. We bathed them. We brushed their hair and fixed their teeth. We worked on reading every night. The biggest thing was that John and I were both there for the children, spent time with them, and loved them in a safe, comfortable, family environment.

Later, when I would look at Jen's long black hair gleaming in the sun or watch Bob's tanned and healthy body as he played like a seal in the swimming pool, I was so grateful we were blessed with the care of these two children.

During their school years I went to the usual parent involvement events, volunteering in the cafeteria and helping on field trips. At some point I was asked by the principals in the elementary and middle schools to teach a class on Native Americans (my children are Native American). I was asked because I had expressed concern about the textbooks portraying all Native Americans incorrectly, and my children were being affected by this misinformation. I wanted them to know about the tribe into which they were born. I served on a Cultural Awareness Committee formed by the superintendent. I did this for four years, until both my son and daughter completed 8th grade. I taught the same kids every year, but changed the lecture to adapt to their grade level.

Our children are 50% Native American from the Choctaw tribe. The Choctaw are one of the Five Civilized Tribes of Oklahoma (Choctaw, Chickasaw, Creek, Seminole and Cherokee). These tribes did not fight the white settlers as they moved into their lands. They worked with the newcomers to divide the land in equal allotments, developed schools, and established local governments. History shows that this worked for a time, but eventually the price they paid for their cooperation was loss of lands, loss of freedom, loss of livelihood, and banishment to the reservations.

When I started the class no one but my children was Native American. After four years the students discovered almost 40% had Native American blood and all of them proud of it. I won the Volunteer of the Year Award from the school district. I became president of the Parent Teacher Organization (PTO) Board for all the schools.

Many times my children were told "no way," but on their own (because *no way* was not in our vocabulary) they succeeded. My son scored the most points in a middle school football game. He was small. He excelled in track and field, won awards for triple jump and hurdles, holds the record at Milford High School for the 400 relay. My daughter played on the basketball team. She was told that, because we transferred from Texas, she was not going to graduate from high school because she was on her last chance to pass the one Ohio test covering history/geography. Guess what? She slam-dunked that test. Because she and mom decided no one says *no way*. Both my children graduated from high school. They told me at their graduations that they thought they would never receive their diploma. I told them that thought never entered my mind.

My children are out on their own now. My son, Bob, is married and he and his super wife have a wonderful baby girl, Auri. My daughter lives close (and remains close) to her brother.

She is a great Aunt "Yen." (Auri can't pronounce her J's yet.) Jen is a wonder at the computer and we call her a lot to fix ours, as mom and dad are not so hot with the computer. One of the best things my kids are doing is that they participate in all sorts of charity events, helping other people whenever they can.

Over the years I have become interested in the environment and developed a Tree Ordinance for the Texas community in which I lived. A participant in starting Keep Southlake Beautiful, we planted 500 trees on each of their campuses with the help of the school children. We cleaned the roadsides two times a year and started the Adopt-A-Road Program. As you can see, one thing led to another as all of these tiny gaps needed someone to get involved, someone to get it started.

I also continued to play soccer. My over-thirty team won North Texas Champions. Why? Because we thought we could win. I played until I was fifty-three and enjoyed every season because I was with a group of women who thought they could win and did win.

For six years I served as president of our Homeowners Association in our neighborhood in Ohio. At every stage of life there are things to be done. I have found *what you need also needs you* is an adage that generally holds true. You can help a great deal by directing your interest and enthusiasm toward whatever calls to you.

My husband and I are retired now. John put his physical plant skills to good use (even though we heard *what can you do after being in a monastery* from more than a few) as he ended up top district Facility Manager in his career with KFC/Pizza Hut, earned a good living, and won many awards. But we still volunteer. Little projects filling little gaps.

So my advice is, take the positive comment and fly with it. Take the negative comment and change it to a positive. Everyone can make a difference. Like a pebble tossed into a lake, the ripples keep spreading. It's bound to help someone, somewhere, sometime, in a positive way.

It's been fifty-four years since I hit the ball out of the ball park because of a negative comment. Oh my, look how far that ripple went. I was reluctant to write this at first, because my generation was taught that talking about your accomplishments indicated a lack of humility. But I have come to believe everyone needs encouragement and inspiration. And these influences often come from the lives of others.

Who said you can't hit a home run? Because I'm here to tell you, *you can.*

Five O

Soyong Kang Partington

Soyong Kang came to this country from South Korea as a young adult. She experienced cultural and other challenges, but her spirit is undaunted and there is a child in her that cannot be squelched. I met her when she was about to marry a friend, Michael Partington. Today, Soyong is an accomplished ceramicist and well-known instructor in the Indianapolis area. She learned additional techniques in raku pottery in South Korea and has accepted an invitation to do some workshops in the Tuscany region of Italy next year. Recently she took up ballroom dancing, but she also plays a mean game of Texas hold 'em. She delights in her children, grandchildren, and a dog named Rufus. Soyong is Life, and I am so happy she agreed to share part of it with us! (Soyong's story is kept in the manner in which she speaks.)

Some say fifty is new forty or even new thirty; it is just another one of those life's chapters to me. I am looking forward to it as a mother, wife, stepmother of five, grandmother of five-so-far, and a ceramic artist.

My first chapter began in Korea as an oldest daughter, sister of two brothers, and mild-tempered good student. My second chapter was having an arranged marriage and giving birth to my daughter just prior to my divorce. The third chapter was to marry again and pursue my passions in life.

As a little girl, one of my dreams was that I want to travel all around the world. I didn't know how, when, and which countries I want to go; but for sure I was going somewhere. We all are made of dreams; without dreams we would not have any destinations.

I have lived in the United States for almost thirty years, which is longer than my life in the country I was born and raised in. December 2, 1981 is the day I came to U.S. from South Korea with my entire family. I was married, pregnant and had only one suitcase. My father, Dr. Yoon Kang, was a physician who decided to come to this country so his three children could get a good education and opportunities in life. Dad could only bring $20,000 into the U.S.A. — the maximum amount he could take from his country back then. He gave up his professional career and fame he had in his whole life. I have to recognize my father's courage before I can even write about myself. We all struggled with language, generation gap, and financial difficulties for many years after immigrating.

My first marriage ended soon after my daughter, Sylvia, was born. Sylvia's father decided that he couldn't deal with cultural differences in the United States and moved back to Korea. It was a family shock when I decided to stay in the States instead of moving back to Korea with my husband. My family didn't want me to be divorced with a one-year-old child.

Miraculously, I convinced them that I could raise a kid on my own.

My first job in the United States was as a waitress. When I told my parents that I will be waiting on tables, my father broke down in tears. He felt like he wasn't providing enough for our family. His old traditional views on waitressing jobs changed when my brothers announced that they too would be working alongside me — to make sure I was never in harm's way.

Later, my father became so proud of me when I finally got a white-collar job, but I still had to keep my second job as a waitress to make ends meet. I also decided to enroll myself in college to study computer science and continued to work 40-50 hours a week while my parents helped with babysitting for Sylvia.

As I worked through those tough years, I stumbled into a community art center — Indianapolis Art Center — and found a ceramic's studio where I can relieve the stress and get back into art. I wanted to study ceramics when I picked my major in Korea, but my parents said that it is not suitable for a woman and told me that I have to choose a major to be landed in a white-collar job. I had to choose to major in graphic design. I remembered how I always enjoyed working with clay in college, so I enrolled myself in a ceramics class, and after a few years, I became an instructor there.

I met Michael at the art center, and we got married and are celebrating ten years of marriage. With his support, I quit my white-collar job and became a full-time ceramic artist.

I received a grant in the amount of $7,500 which is named Creative Renewal Fellowship from Indiana Arts Council in 2001 to go back to Korea to study in Korean Ceramics. After a few months of research, I found out there will be a world event called World Ceramic Expo held in Ichon, Korea, for the very first time. It will be held for three months at three different locations, Ichon, Kwang-Ju, and Yeo-Ju, where pottery techniques have been handed down through generations for over twelve hundred years. I was born and raised in Seoul, Korea, and had only took little tour but knew that these cities are famous producers of Korean Celadon pottery. Also, at this event, there will be the workshops taught by many world famous ceramic artists, including Peter Volkus, Rudy Audio, and Jun Kaneko from the United States, Maria Kuczynska from Poland, Elaine Brant-Hansen from Norway, Ah Leon from Taiwan — about seventy artists from all around the world. What a coincidence that this event will be held just after receiving my grant!

My grant was split — one-half received at the beginning and the rest at the completion. After I purchased my airline ticket, camera and camcorder, and a laptop to help document my experience, the first half of the grant was already spent. I would have to keep my trip to a week or two — if I can find a place to stay with a relative for that long.

Since there is a ten-hour time difference between Indiana and Korea, I stayed up late many nights researching more about the expo event. I made a phone call to the chair of World Ceramic Exposition to see if I can volunteer for a couple of weeks to be involved in this event. He said that the deadline for volunteering had already passed. Disappointed but not giving up yet, I made more phone calls to the local potters council to see if anyone will hire me to stay with them to help in research. The potters I contacted in Korea were surprised to hear such a daring request for a woman—asking to do research in their secrets. I decided to take the different route and called the official manager of the expo's research center, exhibition department and workshops. The manager e-mailed me back and asked for my resume. I e-mailed my resume to him and explained that I'd be willing to work any hours doing any job they needed done. I mentioned my skills as a translator, kiln technician, computer operator and photographer. At that time, I was willing to mop the floor after it was walked on by the world famous artists who were to attend.

Within 24 hours I received a phone call directly from the manager, asking how long I could work for the upcoming event. I said, "Probably a week or two," then added, "I can be there longer if you could provide a place to stay. My expenses may be covered by the potters committee."

He replied, "What else can I say but YES!" I was hired immediately as the expo's workshop coordinator. I'd be contacting the famous guest artists and making sure their workshop visits were a success. My heart was pounding so hard, I could hear it in the phone. As I was writing down what he said, my husband was reading my writing.

When I finished the phone conversation, my eyes were welled up with tears, my whole body was shaking, and I couldn't say anything. When I looked up at my husband, he had both thumbs up for me along with a huge smile. I asked him if it was OK for me to go for a long period of time, and he said "This is a once-in-a-lifetime opportunity; you will be a fool if you don't take it!" I knew then that I had married my soul mate.

A day later I got a phone call about my coordinator responsibilities. They included contacting the most recognizable ceramic artists around the world, inviting them to attend, drawing up the contracts, booking all the hotel reservations, arranging the transportation to and from the airport, providing for the entertainment, arranging meetings with Expo committees and the local potters council, overseeing and managing the public workshops, ordering the materials, overseeing the large kiln firings, and touring the other two official exhibition locations in the country.

The day before I left for my new adventure, I invited my parents for dinner to announce the news. My father was shocked to find out that I will be gone for three months without my husband. His questions were "You will be gone for how long?" "What about your husband?" "How did you decide to quit high paying job then move on to 'dirt' and you called that a career?"

He was really upset and my mother was not helping with the situation. She asked Michael if it was okay with him, then requested, "Tell her not to go, Michael!"

Michael was very confused why they were so negative. He asked my parents, "First of all, do you think she will say 'ok' if I tell her not to go? Do you think she will be happy if she doesn't go? Okay, let's say she didn't go just because I told her not to go. Do you think she will make my life easy?"

Needless to say, I nodded and smiled without jumping into the conversation, thinking again I married the right man who supported my decisions and stood up for them. I invited Michael to come to Korea for three weeks at the end of my three months of work there. It was difficult as the Expo workshop coordinator. I was gone a very long time and I was homesick. While away, we all witnessed 9/11. I didn't know if I would be able to get home —not to mention if Michael could even come to Korea. Michael did make the trip and witnessed me being a strong woman in the middle of all the expo's events.

Just two years after my grant experience in Korea, I lost my father to cancer. I still talk to him daily, though, about my next chapter in life. He manages to give me ideas and inspiration just by knowing he loved me enough to help me start a new life in the U.S.A.

Dollars and Sense

Susan Collins

Susan Collins married young and learned over the years how to manage a home and family finances. She became a saver and a self-taught investor. The middle class created by the Detroit auto industry allowed her husband to provide the comforts of a good income and excellent benefits. They experienced heretofore unheard of developments in quality housing, food, education, shopping, parks and recreation. Susan has worked in clerical and bookkeeping, but as the recession grew and manufacturing jobs were lost, she accepted welfare if necessary to support her loved ones. Susan stretches a dollar better than anyone I know.

During the years we raised our family, the late seventies through early nineties, we never experienced being truly poor or truly wealthy. My husband was blessed with one of the coveted UAW labor positions at a time when benefits were generous and overtime could be counted on. We were scoffed at by some and cursed as highly overpaid by others. We were part of the new middle class created by the auto industry.

I learned the most basic lessons regarding money and how to make the most of it simply by the experience of growing up in a large family. Lessons such as: *used does not mean useless; quality is (truly) more important than quantity;* and *there is always a price to pay and if not clearly stated it is probably too high.* Experience also taught me that it really is nice to pick up the check on occasion, especially if your best friend is loaded. Another: No one likes to be cheated and everyone likes a good deal—even when bartering for Halloween candy.

At the age of sixteen, I hit a parked car and learned all about making a down payment with regular payments to be made. I didn't like it! The concept of an emergency fund was born and tucked away for later in my life.

Financial lessons firmly took hold as part of my personality when, as a young teen, I began waitressing after school hours at the neighborhood Big Boy. During these years, money was often ever present but just as often ever so distant! The total unpredictability of my income while living on tips from day to day taught me to SAVE. When as a young adult I married, and we began our own family, I was prepared to manage our financial matters.

Golden rule #1 was to pay ourselves first by saving from every paycheck. But it hardly began or stopped there. Choices, sacrifices, and saving had to become a family way of life if they were to make a difference in our standard of living.

Beginning at the grocery store, I broke a major rule of most financial advisors by shopping often. However, at a time when coupons were doubled or tripled at the checkout, this method allowed me to shave a substantial amount off my bill. All the clipping and sorting became well worth it as this money was stashed for vacation.

Surprise! My children grew! My daughter and two sons each needed and wanted things! Name brands were so important to them. Providing them with what they wanted on a middle-class income was work. It took many trips to the high-end discount stores or for sale items to consistently purchase the brands they wanted at a fraction of their retail price. Smart shopping allowed me a private smile as I watched those name brands on each of their back pockets as they sauntered off to school. They did not know the low price I had paid; they were simply happy to be sporting the same brands as their peers.

The Great Lakes of Michigan allowed us to take our family on vacation each year without the high cost of airfares. We chose a variety of beach resorts where we met with some of our brothers and sisters and their families, and all enjoyed the rest and relaxation. When we were able to, we occasionally flew to other destinations with our children, or just as a couple.

Often, when the snow and ice hit, with the help of half-off coupons or promotional sales we spent weekends at neighborhood five-star hotels, just to get away. We ate out fancy and spent time sitting in the Jacuzzi, pretending we were anywhere we wanted to be!

When December came, Santa was really, really good to our children. As I look back on these years, I must admit that my brains flew right out the window with the budget at this time of year. I clearly recall standing in a tremendous line with all the other crazy mothers at 6:00 a.m., in the snow, for the absolute privilege of paying the outrageous amount of $45 for a Cabbage

Patch doll. When my turn came, I purchased a doll for my daughter. Spotting a little boy doll, I impulsively purchased it too, for my son. I then spotted a Preemie doll, the rarest and most coveted doll of all that year. I quickly handed over another $45 and thought all the way home how lucky I had been! Spoiling: guilty as charged!

Never could I have anticipated the complete emotional meltdown my daughter experienced when opening her Preemie doll Christmas morning. Barefoot and in PJs, jumping up and down with tears trailing down her cheeks, she ran to her best friend's home to share her joy with her gift. We all laughed and cried as doors opened and faces peeked out to smile at my daughter's hoots and hollers. Santa was never as good as he was that year. It was clear that he had given the entire neighborhood an extra helping of Christmas cheer.

It was, however, blind luck in investing that allowed us to really live differently. When purchasing our first home we never even considered it an investment. We simply wanted a home. Four years later, when we sold it for double what we had paid, it became obvious that it had been a huge and very profitable investment. We put the entire amount of profits down on a larger home, keeping the house payment within our means. Repeating this several times, we soon were able to afford a dream house to raise our family in with a reasonable house payment.

A simple word of caution when investing: BEWARE! Our experiences with other types of investing were not all rosy. While still quite naïve we were introduced to a skilled con artist by a trusted friend. He advised us of strong, good investments.

As our trust grew, he was able to swindle us out of every dime of our cash savings.   Fortunately, most of our financial wealth was safely invested in our home. To avoid this, I suggest investing with a reputable firm, starting small, and doing your homework yourself.

And of course, remember true wealth can not be counted in dollars and cents. We truly loved the family life we had chosen, and it was only with God's constant blessings that we "did it."

The Entrepreneur

Tanja McGuire

Tanja McGuire is one of the new breed of young, energetic, savvy entrepreneurs who found a market niche that had been ignored and pursued it with a passion. On September 11, 2005 she opened a spa and boutique called A Pampered Life on the posh Ocean Drive in Vero Beach. The shop was a smashing success. On February 5, 2010 Tanja hosted the Grand Opening of Polished, a mani-pedi lounge, hair studio and specialty store. "Pampered" and "Polished"...sounds like a winning combination. As you can imagine, this is all rather time consuming. Tanja agreed to be part of my Project, supplying information and approving the results, if I would do the writing. Poof! We had a deal.

When I go to www.apamperedlife.net I find a page bursting with bath and beauty products and services. What draws me in are the soft blue and muted green graphics, but what I zero in on is the little watercolor of Tanja McGuire's shop, *A Pampered Life*. Like Tanja, it is fresh, whimsical, and *au courant*. It looks like a boutique in the middle of Paris, but it's right here in my neighborhood. It makes you want to just hop in the car and drive there!

A Pampered Life is a shower of sights and scents that rain upon you gently as you cross the threshold. Soaps in verbena and lemongrass, lavender and ocean, grapefruit and currant, bamboo and spice; bubble bath fizz, creams and lotions, novelty beauty items, luxurious bathrobes and spa slippers envelop you in a perfumed array of pastel displays.

In contrast, *Polished* is an electric storm of bright colors and bold sensory delights, a jolt of lightning as you enter this new shop on Cardinal Drive. Here can be found the latest in mani-pedi equipment and a hip hair salon, too. Body treatments like massages and facials provided at the Ocean Drive venue are replaced by the latest in nail and hair care, provided in an upscale fashion. Polishes and other accoutrements are in big displays in the reception area. Little samples are available to try. Everything about it seems so…fun.

Tanja McGuire is young, with long blond hair and creamy skin. She is business savvy and full of ideas. Dressed in her signature black smock, Tanja is a bundle of energy as she greets customers, orders product, travels to trade shows, and organizes events. Traveling back and forth daily between both places, it is everything to her to make her visions come to fruition, and they do.

Just thirty-eight (incredibly young by Vero Beach standards), Tanja was born on Pearl Harbor Day and displays the free spirit of Sagittarius. This, she explains, may be part of the reason why she has been known to put her foot in her mouth. The middle child of five girls, she has also been called the Eye of the Storm and believes this accounts for her ability to deal with diverse personalities.

Originally from South Bend Indiana, Home of the Fighting Irish, her background contains plenty of family history with Notre Dame. She has also lived in Louisburg, WV; Memphis, TN; Louisville, KY; Churchville, MD; Jacksonville, FL; Los Angeles, CA; and San Francisco, CA. After a return to LA for a time, she found her home in Vero Beach. A marriage in 1996 ended in divorce in 2007. Looking at the bright side, Tanja counts two children, Maggie and Jack, a father who loves them and is involved in their lives, and her former husband's transfer to Vero when the two were still married, as blessings that led her to this place.

A Pampered Life began as an idea when McGuire first moved to Vero Beach and noticed that Ocean Drive was lacking a bath and beauty boutique that went beyond the traditional hair salon. She scouted a property and began to plan. Almost a year after hurricanes Jeanne and Frances wreaked havoc in Vero Beach, this gutsy proprietor opened her first shop. Choosing a sophisticated black awning with white lettering, an inside theme of dusty green, and black-and-white Victorian print gift bags with pastel shades of tissue paper, customers were immediately drawn into the charm of the new store.

What are some of her secrets for success? Tanja barely hesitates as she lists them. "Surround yourself with people who have the same work ethic and passion for what they do. Look at everything as an inspiration and an opportunity to bring positive things into your life. Take risks but act cautiously — things always work out." Pressed further, she notes that we cannot always control what happens in life but we can control (by our choices) how we react to life's moments. In the end, we can only accomplish what we set out to do daily. There are always obstacles and never enough time. But she has learned how to focus on the priority she sets for the day. Her best advice is sense of humor, sense of humor, sense of humor!

Some amazing things even the casual observer would notice? Her eye for what will sell and a keen sense of products and packaging that will appeal to the upscale market she has come to know. Each spring, an Open House is held so that locals can be privy to new items and expanded services, served up with gourmet food and flowers galore. Seasonal tourists are drawn to the unique gifts, lux bath items and personal services offered in this small oasis—a total spa without the hassle of traveling to some remote retreat. Grandparents, and there are many, find an array of children's items in fun colors, flavors and prints. Young women are offered a vast display of skin care products and makeup. So many small indulgences!

Tanja McGuire is more than an owner-aesthetician, however. She is interested in her customers, receptive to their comments, and open to new ideas. Often seen meeting or talking with fellow business owners, she is supportive of other entrepreneurs and happy to share her thoughts. With two young children, she takes pains to take part in their education and after-school activities. Finally, she recognizes her role in the community and can be seen at various fund-raisers for causes she truly believes in, particularly those concerned with nature and wildlife preservation.

With all this enthusiasm, energy, and involvement, I am not surprised that Tanja McGuire is a success. What surprises me is that she decides to do it again, this time with a place called

Polished. In January of 2005 I receive an invitation to the Grand Opening and Ribbon Cutting Ceremony. Again, it's not just any store opening. It's done with style and panache! The announcement includes Zoya toxin-free nail care, Rene Futurer Paris-essential hair care, jewelry designs from local artists for Dove Plum, and that's not all: "Complimentary Psychic Reading from Debra Hand Psychic Investigator"! Even if you are not tempted to have your fortune told, there is something creative and exciting about it all that draws you to be a part of this event.

On the appointed evening, Tanja and staff are ready. There are tables of strawberry champagne, frosted cupcakes (from a neighboring vendor), tiny sandwiches, and additional catering of food and wine. A festive air predominates, and the feeling of something new and fun and young pervades. The attitude is friendly but fashionable. The influence of this one woman is a breath of fresh air to the wealthy retirement, resistant to development, difficult to change, but beautiful, involved, historical, and resort island town of Vero Beach.

In the quiet of morning store hours a couple of weeks later, Tanja McGuire admits that part of her drive comes from being responsible for "two amazing human beings who will grow to great things." At the end of the day, it is about her children and the comforts of home. Her work is creating a respite for others. Her home is a respite for her family and herself. In Vero Beach, many are simply happy she found a home here.

Too Busy for Bees

Teresa Forshag

*When Teresa Forshag (pronounced **for**-shay) first told me her story we were sitting in her parents' kitchen in Vero Beach, having a cup of tea. Teresa is a pure spirit who pours the energy of heart and soul into everything she does. She didn't want to toot her own horn, doesn't consider herself a writer. And, after sharing the tale of her life's work with me, she told me she was, "too busy for bees." My response was that she had found a title for a book if she ever wrote one. Instead, she agreed to let me write about her and use the title here.*

Teresa Forshag has a life that opens like a flower. Aspects unfold like soft petals. Exotic blooms, plain daisies, fragrant herbs and spices are strewn along her inner garden path. Seeds planted long ago have become seedlings and then fruit bearing trees—a shower of blossoms raining babies, boys, bicycles, and bees.

At the pediatric clinic where Teresa works as a nurse practitioner, several of the children brought in are less than a year old, or newborn, or preemies who require special care, though she deals with children of all ages. Teresa has taken many infants into her home, one at a time, until a foster family can be found. The longest stay was eleven months, but most stay three to four months. So far she has taken in over eighty-five children in almost twenty-one years of foster parenting. She scoffs at the notion this is anything special — they are her "baby fix" and that is that.

It should be noted that there is a clear division between the children Teresa sees in the clinic and those who come to her home. The two never cross. She receives foster placements only through the State (DSHS/CPS). It is important to the well-being of all concerned that she keeps her personal and professional lives independent of one another. So, while the inspiration for one came from the other, and she is very involved in both, they are otherwise unconnected.

Teresa first decided to care for foster babies when she worked as a new nurse in a newborn intensive care unit. She would see some not-so-lovely foster parents come to pick up babies. One woman brought nothing to take Baby home in, just threw (in Teresa's words) her nasty old coat over the infant. The thought crossed her mind that surely she herself could do better than that. Discussing her plan with then fiancé Geoff, she was surprised he didn't run away screaming in the opposite direction, but instead agreed to her plan. She believes he thought this scheme would be implemented *way* in the future. Time passed, the two were wed, and ten months into the marriage the first foster baby arrived. Her husband seemed surprised at this untimely "baby project," but soon they both fell in love with Number One, who became their son Patrick. That was twenty-one years ago.

Because Teresa and her husband had two more children together and were eventually raising three sons, she felt she could not bring older children, victims of unspeakable trauma and horror, into her home. Their sons were her priority and could not be subjected to the trials of her career. But the new babies were loved and cared for during their brief time in the Forshag home, and the Forshag boys became expert at comforting and caring for them. As young boys, they were sure that babies came from the nursery in their home. On many occasions they would peek in and see a newborn in the crib.

"The stork brought another baby!" they would whisper to each other and tiptoe away. As they grew up, the three brothers learned just what to do to bring out a smile or soothe a crying infant. The change-feed-sleep formula became as easy as 1-2-3.

Enjoying a family breakfast at a restaurant one Saturday, middle son Alec, aged four at the time, was asked by a waitress if the baby girl in the infant seat next to him was his little sister.

"No," Alec replied, "she is one of our frosty babies."

Perhaps twelve years later, as the family visited friends who had just brought their newborn baby girl home from the hospital, the tiny creature began to fuss. Alec immediately went over to the bassinette to pick her up.

The new mother, anxiously rising from her chair to protect her daughter from harm, was calmed by Teresa. "Ssh," she said. "Just let him go. He knows what to do."

Picking the baby up gently, careful to hold her downy head, Alec took her in his arms. Cooing to her softly, she quieted in no time. The baby's mother breathed easily again. She looked at Alec and smiled. His mother had taught him well.

Teresa became involved in the foster parent interview process. She wanted to be sure the children were off to a loving home, and she wanted a voice in determining who was chosen to take them. In her basement, on her own dime, she created a room full of baby clothes and accessories. Each child goes with a "dowry" to begin a new life with a new foster family.

Among her duties as an examiner for abused and neglected children, she is charged with documenting case files for the court. Called at any time of the day or night, she is ready to perform her duties, examining little "clients" removed from their homes and taken into protective custody. Her clinic room is more like a playroom, a cheerful place filled with color and cushions, teddy bears and dolls.

Advocacy naturally followed, and Teresa became an expert witness. The court process is precise and painstaking. Everything must be documented without additional trauma to the children. To look at Teresa, a petite blond with gentle eyes and quiet demeanor, you would think a defense attorney could grind her into dust. They don't know she is a formidable opponent, a tower of strength, an advocate for children who have no one. The judges know. The procedure is set in place. She is always called to the witness stand first and asked to state her credentials. It is immediately clear that she knows her stuff. The fight is quickly removed, expertise is firmly established; the defense can stop wasting time and get on with the best interests of the children.

It would be easy to become consumed with this kind of work, but there are other pots brewing in the Forshag household. The family travels extensively and enjoys rugged outdoor camping, hiking, and associated sports. Living in Spokane, Washington, a plethora of natural wonders awaits their exploration and enjoyment. Geoff, a CPA and banker turned business entrepreneur, recently bought an upscale bicycle shop in order to sell mountain bicycles and their accoutrements, and open other price-point possibilities. Living in an area where the green movement is in full swing, biking for sport is big, and people would rather ride than drive to connecting transportation, it seemed like a sound investment.

When the boys became teenagers and needed summer jobs, Geoff purchased or rented the equipment necessary to start a lawn seeding business. The boys learned as they earned. They all had summer jobs. The imagery of sowing seeds became a family affair.

Next, they became interested in raising bees. All five Forshags took a course on how to do just that. They now have several hives in their yard, all the appropriate gear, and bees humming contentedly — and producing honey. What to do with all that golden goo? Why, get it to market, of course. So, added to the other activities and responsibilities of an already busy schedule, Teresa booked space at the local farmers market, bought some jars, and learned to make a commercial enterprise of honey. Some Saturdays she has a baby snuggling against her chest as she chats with neighbors and sells her wares.

Another successful venture is added to the list, even though Teresa Forshag is too busy for bees.

Finding My Strength

Tiffany Vincent

At first glance, Tiffany Vincent may strike someone as the girl who has everything. Tall, with a sleek body and long legs, straight blond hair streaming off her shoulders or up in a French twist, dressed in jeans or perhaps a jade green sundress, she could be on the cover of a magazine. On break from university in the summer, she works as a lifeguard at a suburban country club, which looks, perhaps, like just more glamour. In fact, she has dealt with some adult issues, handled difficult situations without bothering her friends, and grown from a girl to a mature woman through trying circumstances. Tiffany's forte is the written word, and it was through her notes and letters that I realized she may initially appear shallow on the surface, but she is truly still water that runs deep.

There are certain moments when you can feel it in the air that something bad is coming. You try and convince yourself that it's all in your head, your imagination getting the best of you; and just when you seem to have put the chill-bearing thoughts in the back of your head, you hear that sob that cuts the air like a bullet and your stomach drops.

My mother came barreling down the stairs, so distraught that her cries were no longer audible and all she could seem to do was focus on trying to breathe. I sat at the computer, my heart racing and my eyes welling with tears, staring at someone I could hardly believe to be the mother I knew. As minutes that felt as long as hours passed, she managed to repress the seemingly uncontrollable sobs long enough to tell me to pack a bag. I didn't even think to ask why or where we were going; I simply went upstairs and threw some clothes into a bag and made my way to the car.

That night we stayed at a close family friend's house; my mother tucked herself away in the basement and continued to fall apart. It wasn't until the following morning that she brought herself to tell me what had happened.

For the past eight years my mother had been married to my stepfather, whose name I feel is not worth mentioning. I recall the first few months they were together, my mother was so happy, and for this reason alone I went along with the moving into his house, changing schools, and making a new family. If I had known then what he would do to her, I never would have tolerated it so kindly. Nonetheless, after years of a seemingly happy marriage, things began to turn. The night my mother came sobbing down the stairs, she had asked my stepfather if he loved her. It was that night that he looked her dead in the eyes and simply said *no*. Neither of us knew at the time, though my mother had her suspicions, that my stepfather was indeed having an affair with some woman from his work. The day my mother's divorce was finalized was the same day her husband of eight years eloped to Las Vegas.

The days that followed are a blur. I took a few days off from school as my mother and I moved into a one bedroom apartment for the remainder of my senior year in high school. I remember our first night in the apartment; my mother had divulged to me that we had thirteen dollars until she got her next paycheck in a few days and that things might be tight for a while. So we got Chinese food and ate it among our boxes in silence. I went back to school the next day and put myself on auto pilot. I went from class to class with a smile on my face, laughed at lunch with friends and went to volleyball practice. There were a few friends I allowed to know what was going on — the few I knew wouldn't grimace when they found out I was living in a one bedroom apartment with my mother. Other than those few friends, I made sure my life at school remained relatively the same.

It was at home that I couldn't pretend things were okay. I watched as my mother became ill from her depression. Her body wouldn't allow her to eat and her mind wouldn't allow her to sleep. As her condition worsened she was forced to see a doctor, who required she not work for a while. I will never forget the night I was at my friend's house and received a voicemail on my phone from my mother. She informed me that she was in the hospital and had to call an ambulance for herself because she couldn't breathe. This entire scene happened more than once. My mother continued having serious health problems and was forced to have heart surgery.

At age eighteen, I had seen my mother's heart broken.

There are days when I still get mad about what happened, when I drive past the street where we had all lived together or something reminds me of it all. However, as I look and talk with my mother now and see her smiling and laughing, moving up in her career and being asked out on dates, I realize I would take none of it back. My mother and I have never been closer; we were forced to go through something together that was bigger than we were at the time. But now that we made it through the darkness, I find we are better for it and less afraid about what the big bad world has to offer.

While my mother chose to start her life over again in Virginia, I have remained in East Lansing and am currently working on putting myself through school at Michigan State University. I am now the hardworking, self-reliant college student full of promise for tomorrow. (Who, I must admit, dreams of creating a line of lipsticks called *lippity slicks*.)

When I think of modern women, I think of all the things women have accomplished over the years, what they have fought for and what we have now. It all takes strength, and this is what I see in my mother. She fought for herself and she fought for me. She managed to pick herself up off the floor and make our relationship stronger out of it all, to embrace life and live it to the fullest. Such stories as my mother's are too often typical of the lives of today's women, but they set a fine standard for those of us who are fortunate enough to have such stalwart role models. I couldn't be happier I had such a good—and strong—example to learn from.

It made me realize my own strength.

What Color Do You Want to Be?

Jennifer Suzanne Boyce

Jennifer is my sister, the last sibling in our tribe of twelve children. I was away at college when she was born, and she could not fathom how I fit into the family. "Why is she calling you 'Mom,'?" she would ask my mother. And, "Why is she always bringing me presents?" when I arrived with a book or a toy for the little sister I barely knew. It was disconcerting, to say the least. Though we come from the same brood, we are in fact a generation apart. I hesitated to include her essay at first, which – typical for Jen – was submitted beyond late, but something struck me about the different problems of her age group. Thirty-somethings today are dealing with issues I never experienced: ADD (Attention Deficit Disorder), OCD (Obsessive Compulsive Disorder) and related learning and psychological challenges; job loss and fierce competition for limited professional jobs; online matchmaking, broken romances, and difficulty in finding lasting relationships; and staggering financial debt from credit cards and student loans. But it's not all bleak, as Jennifer is here to tell you. She's going in last but not – by far – least.

Life is surprising to say the least. Just when I think I have it all figured out, something changes and I am amazed. I am amazed at the power of love, the strength of the human spirit, and the wisdom of the young and old. I was the twelfth and last child born to Robert and Beverly Boyce. I was born on my due date, September 27, 1973, yet I have struggled with timeliness ever since.

In December of 2001 I was 28, living single, in love with my college sweetheart, and working as a counselor at a local non-profit. I had finished my master's degree earlier that year and everything seemed to be falling into place. Money was tight but life was good.

Two years passed and the tides took a turn for the worse. I had lost my low-paying but professional job and tried to pay the rent with a couple of waitressing jobs. I pulled and pulled and still my ends did not meet. I swallowed my pride and asked my sister Michelle if I could live in her basement for "maybe six months or so" until I could get back on my feet again. She and her husband agreed…and six months turned into eighteen. I had been so determined to survive on my own that I hadn't even asked them until I had about one week to either vacate my apartment or renew a lease that I could not afford.

Michelle smiled and asked, "What was your plan if we had said no?"

"I don't know," I said, "I didn't have a plan B." She had figured as much, so she wasn't surprised. Since we are closest in age, she knows me better than most. I figured our new living arrangement would either make or break us. Luckily, we didn't break.

In the first week of 2004 I moved in with Michelle, Joe, and their three young children: Robert, Grace and Matthew. It was a great experience for me and we all got along well. I was able to develop a deeper relationship with all of them and at the same time be a helping hand with the kids. We would joke that the 1:1 adult-child ratio made life easier for them. I enjoyed being a part of their busy household.

Time went on and I began to become somewhat isolated. I was feeling anxious and depressed about my job situation, and was also suffering from Obsessive Compulsive Disorder (OCD). OCD is an anxiety disorder that makes living in the moment very difficult. I had begun treatment in the form of medication and counseling in 1999. Since the loss of my job, I had not been taking my medication due to financial limitations, and slowly my thoughts were taken up by excessive and often irrational worry.

Symptoms vary from person to person. I struggled with an overload of thoughts. We all have many thoughts every second, but with OCD it is as if you can't prioritize and/or dismiss unnecessary thoughts. I would feel confused, anxious, tired, and often afraid. I would sometimes fear I was losing my mind. I worried when I stuck my foot in my mouth that I would be disliked, which would lead me to replay situations over and over in my head. Then I would worry that I had wasted time thinking about nonsense and that I was just plain weird. I worried about loved ones, and checked that the doors were locked three or four or five times in a row. My anxiety at times would be paralyzing and painful, both emotionally and physically. This would cause me to isolate from others and sleep —a lot.

When an individual suffers from OCD, he/she develops self-soothing behaviors to cope. I would shower and sleep excessively because both were calming and an avoidance of anxious situations. One day stands out in my memory. It was around ten o'clock on a summer morning. I was in bed in my basement hideaway. I was awake, in the fetal position, and could feel increasing tightness in my chest and stomach. I heard the door open at the top of the stairs, the stairway light was turned on, followed by the pitter-patter of little feet coming down the stairs. Then I heard young Robert's voice.

"Aunt Jenny?" he inquired.

I rolled over toward him and mumbled, "Yeah buddy, what do you need?"

"We want to play LIFE," he said, referring to the board game.

"All right...do you need me to get it out of the closet?"

"No, I got it down. Can I set it up on the floor in the family room?"

I was not sure why he was involving me in this decision-making process, but I thought perhaps my sister was on the phone and he wanted an adult to give him permission to make a mess. So I responded, "Sure, sounds good." Then I reminded him to turn the light off. Approximately ten minutes later I heard the door open upstairs again. The light was turned on, and then came the pitter-patter.

Robert was once again standing at the foot of my bed saying, "Aunt Jenny?"

I sighed and in a slightly irritated tone, for the second time that morning asked, "What do you need?"

After a brief pause he asked sweetly, "What color do you want to be?"

My irritation melted away as I realized my nephew was not looking for assistance, permission to make a mess, or an opportunity to annoy his sleeping aunt. He was simply asking me to play a game and had been patiently waiting for me to join him. He didn't need me — ironically, I needed him. His innocent persistence gave me the strength to join the living that day. We walked up the stairs together and I thought, *Okay, I get it God. Get up and play the game of life!*

I believe God places us all on a journey. Life is often uncomfortable and sometimes painful, but we need to keep living, loving and learning. And that is precisely what I decided to do.

Soon after that day, I went back to the doctor and on medication with financial help from my family. My mother and many of my siblings had given me loans or financial help at one time or another and I will forever be grateful. I started "working" for an elderly woman, Lucinda (Lucy), who was suffering from terminal cancer. My friend Lauren recommended me to Lucy, who had been a dear friend for many years. Lucy's husband, John, had recently died, and she was having a hard time with maintaining her home, plus she didn't drive. We had agreed on an hourly wage, and she paid me for my time at the end of each day in cash. It didn't take long for us to become friends. She was a feisty little redhead, albeit an artificial redhead by the time I met her in her eighties! I did light cleaning, took out the garbage, made her lunch and kept her company.

My daily tasks gradually consisted of less cleaning and more conversing. She told me about important people and events in her life, and I was able to get back on my feet while learning some valuable life lessons. Lucy told me about the death of her parents when she was a child and her often loveless upbringing in an orphanage. She spoke about how her childhood made her bitter and pushed her away from her faith in God. She described various struggles in her adulthood and how she dealt with them. But more than anything else, she spoke about her wonderful husband. I learned that they had been friends for several years and had both struggled to overcome similar demons in their lives. At some point their feelings grew into a romance and they were married for forty-some years. Lucy and John had married in their late thirties and had only one daughter, who, sadly, was stillborn. I heard about arguments, forgiveness, grief and healing.

John was a devout Catholic but Lucy explained that he never forced his religion upon her. However, the way he lived his life was an example of true faith and love. His example rekindled the faith in God she held within, and she started attending church.

I knew Lucy for only six months. The day she died I looked up as I was driving on my way to the hospice to grieve with friends. The sky was a pale blue with vibrant red streaks as the sun was setting. Living in Detroit doesn't allow for many sunsets, but that day I felt Lucy's presence and I knew she was fine. Her red hair was illuminating the heavens!

I am now nearing my thirty-seventh birthday. I've experienced love, break-ups, heartache, grief, despair, humility, hope and even happiness. I currently have all I need and am working in my field. I have been dating and hoping to find a love to last a lifetime. My parents showed me that true love not only exists but can overcome life's sorrows and disappointments. They raised twelve children and never lacked love for any one of us or for each other. I also know that true love can happen later in life and actually bring out one's inner beauty and strength, because God allowed me to meet a very special redhead.

We are all playing the Game of Life and the roll of the dice brings different opportunities for each of us. The wonderful part about this is that the board is the same for everyone, but the possibilities are limitless. What color do you want to be?

LaVergne, TN USA
08 November 2010
203960LV00002B/3/P